United States
Department of
Agriculture

Forest Service

Pacific Northwest
Research Station

General Technical
Report
PNW-GTR-829
November 2010

Land Use Planning Ballot Initiatives in the Pacific Northwest

Technical Editors

Jeffrey D. Kline is a research forester, Forestry Sciences Laboratory, 3200 SW Jefferson Way, Corvallis, OR 97331; and **Eric M. White** is a research associate, Department of Forest Engineering, Resources and Management, College of Forestry, Oregon State University, 3200 SW Jefferson Way, Corvallis, OR 97331.

Cover photo

Eric White.

Land Use Planning Ballot Initiatives in the Pacific Northwest

Jeffrey D. Kline and Eric M. White, Technical Editors

U.S. Department of Agriculture
Forest Service
Pacific Northwest Research Station
General Technical Report PNW-GTR-829
November 2010

Abstract

Kline, Jeffrey D.; White, Eric M., tech. eds. 2010. Land use planning ballot initiatives in the Pacific Northwest. Gen. Tech. Rep. PNW-GTR-829. Portland, OR: U.S. Department of Agriculture, Forest Service, Pacific Northwest Research Station. 55 p.

Sustaining farm and forest land has been an important goal in the United States because of the role these lands play in the livelihoods of rural residents while also providing desired open space benefits. However, land use policies to protect rural lands often involve a tension between balancing public interests regarding economic and open space goals with the private interests and property rights of farm and forest land owners. This tension is especially prevalent when policies involve the regulation of private land such as through land use planning. In the Pacific Northwest, where statewide planning has been enacted in both Oregon and Washington, that tension is manifested in periodic voting on ballot initiatives and referenda seeking to either strengthen or weaken existing planning policies. The voting outcomes of these initiatives and referenda provide insights into how and why voters value farm and forest lands, and how voters feel about the degree to which private landowners should contribute to their protection. In this report, we present two studies of voting patterns from ballot measures in Oregon and Washington intended to modify land use planning regulations in those states. The studies portray the complex nature of voters' perceptions and preferences of the advantages and disadvantages of regulating land use. The picture that emerges may help policymakers, government officials, and organizations interested in land use policies reconcile the seemingly contradictory nature of voter behavior in land use planning ballot initiatives.

Keywords: Land use planning and policy, development, voting, referenda, and ballot initiatives.

Contents

1 **Chapter 1: Introduction**
   Jeffrey D. Kline and Eric M. White

2 **Oregon Land Use Planning**

4 **Washington Land Use Planning**

5 **The Studies**

6 **References**

9 **Chapter 2: Washington and Oregon's Socioeconomic Landscape and the Impact on Land Use Referenda Voting**
   Juli S. Kim and Eric M. White

9 **Introduction**

10 **Measure 37 and Initiative 933**

13 **Legal Challenges**

13 **M37 and I933 Opposition**

17 **M37 and I933 Support**

19 **Methods**

19 Empirical Approach

21 Explanatory Variables

23 Estimated Models

23 **Results**

28 **Discussion**

30 **Conclusions**

31 **References**

35 **Chapter 3: The Influence of Measure 37 Claims on Voting Shifts Between Measure 37 and Measure 49**
   Garrett Chrostek

35 **Introduction**

36 **Land Use Policy in Oregon**

39 **Literature Review**

42 **Data, Hypotheses, and Methods**

45 **Results**

45 County-Level Models

48 Precinct-Level Models

51 **Conclusions and Policy Implications**

53 **Acknowledgments**

54 **References**

Chapter 1: Introduction

Jeffrey D. Kline and Eric M. White

Sustaining farm and forest land has long been viewed as an important goal in the United States because of the role these land use activities play in the livelihoods of rural residents. Increasingly, rural lands also are valued for the role they play in providing open space benefits—watershed protection, fish and wildlife habitat, and outdoor recreation opportunities, among others—that play a critical role in sustaining our psychological health and ethical relationship to the nonhuman world (Gobster 2004). However, despite these underlying motivations, public policies to protect rural lands often bring about tension associated with balancing public interests regarding open space with the private interests of owners of farm and forest land. This tension is especially prevalent when policies involve the regulation of private land for public gain. Disagreement about how to reconcile the protection of socially desired land uses while maintaining the sanctity of private property rights is as persistent as it is common in the United States. Improving our understanding of how the public views rural lands protection policies and how those policies affect private landowners is a necessary step in fostering effective approaches to rural land protection that minimize conflict.

Understanding of how the public views rural lands protection policies and how those policies affect private landowners is a necessary step in fostering effective approaches to rural land protection.

The collective action of voters in supporting or opposing land use restrictions on private land can provide insights regarding how and why society values particular rural land uses, such as forestry and farming, as well as the degree to which society believes private landowners should contribute to protection. Information about the socioeconomic and demographic factors and landscape characteristics influencing collective behavior regarding the protection of rural lands can provide information needed for understanding the public's support for formulating public policy and natural resource management actions. A common way to examine collective action regarding rural lands protection is with voting data from public referenda intended to implement various land use policies and restrictions (e.g., Deacon and Shapiro 1975, Kahn and Matsusaka 1997, Kline and Armstrong 2001, Kline and Wichelns 1994, Kotchen and Powers 2006, Press 2003, Salka 2003, Solecki et al. 2004). These studies show that a variety of socioeconomic and demographic factors (e.g., income, education) and land characteristics (e.g., prevailing land use, open space scarcity) correlate with voting outcomes regarding land use policies. Although their conclusions offer few definitive factors or proof of the reasons for voting behavior, analyses of voting patterns do provide an empirical foundation from which to consider and speculate about what particular outcomes mean.

This report presents studies examining voting patterns in Oregon and Washington regarding ballot measures intended to modify land use planning regulations in those states. In the first study, Kim and White examined voting patterns observed from Measure 37 in Oregon and Initiative 933 in Washington, both of which sought to provide compensation to landowners for losses in property value that may have resulted from imposed land use restrictions. In the second study, Chrostek examined differences in voting patterns in Oregon between Measure 37 and the subsequent Measure 49, which sought to restore many of the protections seemingly undone by Measure 37. Together, the two studies portray the complex nature of voters' perceptions and preferences as they weigh the advantages and disadvantages of land use planning. We hope the picture that emerges enables policymakers, government officials, and organizations interested in land use policy to better understand and anticipate voters' likely responses to future land use policy initiatives, as well as reconcile the seemingly contradictory nature of voter behavior regarding land use planning ballot initiatives.

Oregon Land Use Planning

Oregonians long have had a strong connection to the natural resources in their state. Oregon's forest and agricultural lands historically have been recognized as among the most productive in the United States, and have provided significant employment in those sectors. More recently, Oregonians have been found to have high levels of concern for the environment. In one survey, for example, Oregonians placed high values on clean air and water, and the protection of wilderness and wildlife—they viewed noneconomic forest values as more important than economic values (Davis and Hibbits, Inc. 1999). Moreover, Oregonians have some of the highest levels of participation in outdoor recreation in the Nation (Cordell 2004). These trends seem to indicate a populace that recognizes the productive capacity of its landscape and its contribution to the state's economic well-being while also recognizing a variety of other landscape benefits that warrant protection.

These multiple interests are acknowledged in the several stated goals that define Oregon's land use planning program. Enacted in 1973 with Senate Bill 100 and fully implemented by the mid-1980s, Oregon's statewide system of land use planning seeks to protect rural lands for forest and agricultural uses, and environmental resources of particular note, while enabling the urban growth necessary to accommodate a growing population and economy. The program required all cities and counties to prepare comprehensive land use plans consistent with several statewide goals, including the orderly and efficient transition of rural lands to urban uses, the protection of forests and agricultural lands, and the protection and conservation of natural resources, scenic and historical areas, and open spaces that "promote a healthy environment and natural landscape" (DLCD 2004: 1). To advance these goals, cities and counties are required to focus new development inside urban-growth boundaries and to restrict development outside of urban-growth boundaries by zoning those lands for exclusive farm or forest use, or as exception areas (Pease 1994). Exception areas are unincorporated rural areas where low-density residential, commercial, and industrial uses prevail, and where development is allowed, pending approval by local authorities (Einsweiler and Howe 1994).

Since its inception, Oregon's Land Use Planning Program has created tension between its advocates, who see land use planning as necessary to the long-term conservation of forest and farm lands, and its detractors who argue that land use regulations unduly burden private landowners (Oppenheimer 2004a, 2004b). This tension periodically is played out in ballot measures that seek to alter land use planning in the state. Despite curtailing some individual private property rights, Senate Bill 100 initially was met with the general support of the state's citizens at the time of passage, including many in the agricultural community. However, over time, opposition to land use planning has organized and grown. Measure 7, which called for compensating private landowners for reductions in the market value of their property, was passed by voters in 2000. Measure 7 was subsequently overturned by the Oregon Supreme Court on a technicality, but its general intent reemerged with Measure 37 in 2004. Passing with 61 percent of the vote, Measure 37 accomplished two things: (1) it lowered the threshold for making claims for regulatory takings, and (2) it established a new avenue for relief from administrative rules that limited activities on private lands via compensation for reductions in value or waiving of regulations. A worry among land use planning officials was that few government jurisdictions would be in a financial position to very often compensate landowners who filed claims.

To both clarify and alter the Measure 37 result, the State legislature voted to put a proposed amendment to Measure 37 (Measure 49) to the voters in 2007. Measure 49 significantly curtailed rules mandated by Measure 37 and passed with 61 percent of the vote. The primary changes to Measure 37 mandated by Measure 49 were that administrative relief was not granted for restrictions on industrial or commercial development on high-value farm or forest lands, development on land designated as critical groundwater areas, and for development involving subdivisions of more than 10 houses. Ultimately, Measure 49 did not completely nullify Measure 37, but it did significantly weaken the earlier measure by limiting potential compensation and vastly reducing the number of eligible claimants.

Like residents in many Western States, Oregonians place much emphasis on maintaining the rights of individuals both in terms of personal rights as well as the individual role in effecting government policies. As to the rights of the individual in the legislative process, Oregon has a biennial legislative session, in part, to promote the citizen legislator, a progressive vote-by-mail election system, and a well-used system for putting public referenda before voters. Oregon's public referendum system dates to 1902 and was enacted to ensure the power of citizens to enact legislation (Oregon State Archives 2009). To be put to a vote, proposed legislation must obtain a requisite number of voter signatures equal to a fixed percentage of the number of votes cast in the previous general election. In addition to legitimizing legislation developed by citizens, the referendum system also allows the legislature to put proposed legislation to the voters, as was the case with Measure 49. Since 1902, more than 800 pieces of legislation have been put to a vote before the Oregon electorate, with slightly fewer than 50 percent passing (Oregon State Archives 2009).

Land use planning regulations in Oregon also must be considered within the context of land use patterns and ownership in the state. About half of Oregon is in federal ownership. In the eastern part of the state, federal ownerships generally cover large contiguous portions of the landscape, whereas in the western part of the state, the landscape is more often a patchwork of mixed federally owned and private lands, reflecting the historical pattern of land settlement there. Federal ownership of lands is least common in the Willamette Valley, which extends from Eugene in the south to Portland in the north. Across all ownerships, forest land accounts for 48 percent of the landscape (Smith and others 2004). Of nonfederal lands, forest land accounts for about 41 percent of land, with crop, pasture, and rangeland accounting for 50 percent. About 4 percent of the nonfederal landscape is in urban and developed uses, making Oregon one of the least developed states in the Nation (USDA NRCS 2000).

Washington Land Use Planning

Statewide land use planning in Washington lagged Oregon's program by almost 20 years. Washington's legislature passed the Growth Management Act in 1990 to reduce urban sprawl, concentrate urban growth, support property rights, and conserve lands important to the state's agriculture and forest industries (Washington State Department of Community, Trade, and Economic Development 2006). Under Washington's growth management program, most county governments are responsible for developing countywide comprehensive land use plans and regularly updating them. These comprehensive plans and their associated zoning regulations form the approximate boundaries of future land use and land use change within the counties. Urban-growth boundaries must be delineated sufficient in size to accommodate the majority of expected future populations. To protect rural landscapes for natural resource industries, the growth management program requires counties to designate long-term commercially important agriculture, forest, or mineral areas as "designated resource lands," on which allowable development is significantly curtailed. By 2000, most local governments in Washington had completed their initial comprehensive plans, and, by the end of 2007, most had completed their first mandated comprehensive plan revisions (Washington State Department of Community, Trade, and Economic Development 2006).

Similar to the Oregon experience, land use planning in Washington has inspired debate about the appropriate balance of regulation and public interest, culminating most recently in Initiative 933. Similar to Measure 37 in Oregon, Initiative 933 in Washington sought to extend compensation to private landowners whose property value was reduced by environmental or other land use regulations mandated by state or local governments. Also like Measure 37, Initiative 933 lacked any funding mechanism for compensating landowners, and it was expected that most government entities would waive land use regulations subject to claims. Washington voters ultimately rejected Initiative 933 in 2006 with 59 percent voting "no." Some observers speculated that Oregon's experience with Measure 37 may have swayed voters against Initiative 933. Whether true or not, the Initiative 933 outcome provides yet another opportunity to consider what factors might contribute to public perceptions and preferences regarding land use policy as revealed through voting.

The Studies

The studies featured in the remaining two chapters of this report were completed separately but complement each other by providing two different analyses of voting regarding Pacific Northwest land use policies. In the second chapter, Kim and White examine voting on Measure 37 in Oregon and the subsequent Initiative 933 in Washington within the context of changing socioeconomic, demographic, and employment patterns in both states. The chapter begins with a description of proposed legislation and advocacy leading up to votes on ballot measures, including legal challenges. Regression models are developed to examine the degree of support for each measure relative to socioeconomic, demographic, and employment factors, voters' political affiliation, and landscape characteristics hypothesized to influence voting patterns. Regression results of the models are discussed in the context of other literature and the past and expected future demographic changes in both states.

The third chapter extends the voting analysis described in the second chapter by examining changes in voting patterns between Measure 37 and its follow-up Measure 49. In that chapter, Chrostek describes the reactions of various government agencies and advocacy groups to Measure 37 during the years following its passage, including the creation of the Big Look Task Force to examine land use and land use planning in Oregon and the placement of the subsequent Measure 49 on the ballot. Regression models are estimated to examine the shift in voter support between Measures 37 and 49. The regression results are used to test several hypotheses regarding possible explanations for passage of Measure 37, which was intended to limit Oregon land use planning, but then later passage of Measure 49, which restored many of the powers limited by Measure 37. Conclusions from the study provide several policy implications and identify opportunities for research.

Although neither study offers a definitive explanation for individual voter behavior on any of the ballot measures examined, the studies do help to identify many of the factors that might weigh on the minds of voters as they try to reconcile public interest with private property rights through the voting process. Qualitative and quantitative analyses provide a picture of how voters respond to different types of information put forth by advocacy groups on opposing sides of the land use policy debate. Moreover, the regression models identify specific socioeconomic, demographic, and other factors useful in anticipating and understanding future voting outcomes.

> **The studies do help to identify many of the factors that might weigh on the minds of voters as they try to reconcile public interest with private property rights through the voting process.**

References

Cordell, H.K. 2004. Outdoor recreation for 21st century America. State College, PA: Venture Publishing. 293 p.

Davis and Hibbits, Inc. 1999. Oregonians discuss forest values, management goals, and related issues. Portland, OR: Oregon Forest Resources Institute. 19 p.

Deacon, R.; Shapiro, P. 1975. Private preference for collective goods revealed through voting on referenda. American Economic Review. 65(5): 943–955.

Department of Land Conservation and Development [DLCD]. 2004. Oregon's statewide planning goals and guidelines. Salem, OR. http://www.oregon.gov/LCD/goals.shtml. (July 20, 2009).

Einsweiler, R.C.; Howe, D.A. 1994. Managing "the land between": a rural development paradigm. In: Abbott, C.; Howe, D.; Adler, S., eds. Planning the Oregon way. Corvallis, OR: Oregon State University Press: 245–274.

Gobster, P.H. 2004. Introduction: the social aspects of landscape change: protecting open space under pressure of development. Landscape and Urban Planning. 69(2-3): 149–151.

Kahn, M.E.; Matsusaka, J.G. 1997. Demand for environmental goods: evidence from voting patterns on California initiatives. Journal of Law and Economics. 40(1): 137–173.

Kline, J.D.; Armstrong, C. 2001. Autopsy of a forestry ballot initiative: characterizing voter support for Oregon's Measure 64. Journal of Forestry. 99(5): 20–27.

Kline, J.; Wichelns, D. 1994. Using referendum data to characterize public support for purchasing development rights to farmland. Land Economics. 70(2): 223–233.

Kotchen, M.J.; Powers, S.M. 2006. Explaining the appearance and success of voter referenda for open-space conservation. Journal of Environmental Economics and Management. 52: 373–390.

Oppenheimer, L. 2004a. Initiative reprises land battle. Portland Oregonian. September 20; http://www.oregonlive.com/printer/printer.ssf?/base/news/1095681480156700.xml. (March 25, 2005).

Oppenheimer, L. 2004b. The people: landowners take sides on Measure 37. Portland Oregonian. October 7; http://www.oregonlive.com/printer/printer.ssf?/base/news/109715027827560.xml. (March 25, 2005).

Oregon State Archives. 2009. Oregon blue book: initiative, referendum, and recall introduction. Salem, OR; http://bluebook.state.or.us/state/elections/elections09.htm. (April 9, 2009).

Pease, J.R. 1994. Oregon rural land use: policy and practices. In: Abbott, C.; Howe, D.; Adler, S., eds. Planning the Oregon way. Corvallis, OR: Oregon State University Press: 163–188.

Press, D. 2003. Who votes for natural resources in California? Society and Natural Resources. 16(9): 835–846.

Salka, W.M. 2003. Determinants of countywide voting behavior on environmental ballot measures: 1990–2000. Rural Sociology. 68(2): 253–277.

Solecki, W.D.; Mason, R.J.; Martin, S. 2004. The geography of support for open-space initiatives: a case study of New Jersey's 1998 ballot measure. Social Science Quarterly. 85(3): 624–639.

Smith, B.W.; Miles, P.D.; Vissage, J.S.; Pugh, S.A. 2004. Forest resources of the United States. Gen. Tech. Rep. NC-241. St. Paul, MN: U.S. Department of Agriculture, Forest Service, North Central Research Station. 137 p.

U.S. Department of Agriculture, Natural Resources Conservation Service [USDA NRCS]. 2000. Table 1 Surface area of nonfederal and federal land and water areas, by state and year (data per 1,000 acres). http://www.nrcs.usda.gov/TECHNICAL/NRI/1997/summary_report/table1.html. (June 22, 2007).

Washington State Department of Community, Trade, and Economic Development. 2006. Creating liveable communities: managing Washington's growth for 15 years. Olympia, WA; http://www.cted.wa.gov/_CTED/documents/ID_3175_Publications.pdf. (April 9, 2009).

Chapter 2: Washington and Oregon's Socioeconomic Landscape and the Impact on Land Use Referenda Voting

Juli S. Kim[1] and Eric M. White

Introduction

On November 2, 2004, Oregon voters passed ballot Measure 37 (M37), a property rights initiative, with 61 percent voting "yes." This measure required state and local governments to compensate or waive regulations for property owners when regulations restricted the usage of or devalued their property. Two years later, a similar measure, Initiative 933 (I933), was opposed, with 59 percent voting "no" in neighboring Washington state. The different outcomes in two seemingly similar states raises questions about what factors influence the voting patterns pertaining to land use policy and natural resource management. Although many of the major tenets of M37 were later modified in November 2007 with the passage of Oregon's Measure 49, understanding and comparing the influences that shaped the voting patterns in the adjacent state that shares a strong history of legislative action aimed at conserving natural resources could assist in gaining a better understanding of voter behavior; assist state legislators and natural resource planners to anticipate, respond to, and plan for constituent preferences; and perhaps even avoid the legislative back-and-forth that ensued with M37.

This paper documents voting patterns observed in Oregon and Washington when private-property rights initiatives arose to modify existing land use planning legislation.

Both states have experienced changing socioeconomic and demographic landscapes that could preface a shift in public opinion on issues such as land use and natural resource management. These changes have mainly been driven by population growth and inmigration from other states. Some of the most obvious trends include increased population and the expansion of urban areas. This paper documents voting patterns observed in Oregon and Washington when private-property rights initiatives arose to modify existing land use planning legislation. Using multiple regression, we examine support and opposition to M37 and I933 as a function of socioeconomic, demographic, and landscape characteristics, and highlight changes in population characteristics that could correspond to changing constituent desires in the future.

[1] Juli S. Kim was a career intern with the Cooperative Forestry Staff, State and Private Forestry, U.S. Department of Agriculture, Forest Service, 1400 Independence Ave SW, mailstop 1123, Washington, DC 20250-1123.

Comparing voting patterns in Oregon and Washington on legislation limiting land use regulations is especially fitting because these two states have consistently had some of the Nation's most formalized state-level planning laws. In addition, both states have a progressive electoral system. Since 1998, every vote in Oregon has been conducted via a vote-by-mail system, and in Washington, 37 out of 39 counties currently vote by mail. The analysis we conduct here also recognizes the time between passage of M37 in Oregon and voting in Washington on I933. Because the two states are adjacent and there was extensive local media coverage of the controversies surrounding M37 landowner claims, it seems likely that the impacts on Oregon post-M37 had an influence on Washingtonians' voting behavior on I933.

Measure 37 and Initiative 933

Ballot initiatives related to property owner compensation for government-imposed land use planning regulations first appeared in the early 1990s, when states such as Florida, Louisiana, Mississippi, and Texas passed property-rights laws to protect landowners from monetary losses caused by zoning. However, none of these was broadly written, and none had a significant impact on local land use regulation (Harden 2005). By comparison, M37 was broadly written, extending the term "damage" to refer to any amount or degree of restriction, setting in place a retroactive claims mechanism, allowing owners to submit claims for regulations adopted in the years since they acquired their property, and allowing waivers in cases where the government could not compensate owners for damages from land use restrictions.

After M37's passage in Oregon, many similar initiatives sprang up throughout the West. In 2006, voters in six Western States considered ballot initiatives similar to Oregon's M37: Arizona—Proposition 207, California—Proposition 90, Idaho—Proposition 2, Montana—Initiative 154, Nevada—State Question 6, and Washington—I933. With the exception of Arizona, voters in all of these states rejected the initiatives. Amongst the 2006 initiatives, I933 was the most similar to M37.

Measure 37 was sponsored by Oregonians in Action (OIA), a nonprofit group whose main goal is "fighting for property rights and against excessive land use regulations" (OIA, n.d.). Initiative 933 was sponsored by the Washington State Farm Bureau, a voluntary grassroots advocacy organization representing the "social and economic interests of farm and ranch families" (Washington Farm Bureau 2008). Both initiatives were property-rights initiatives that would have entitled landowners whose property value was reduced by environmental or other land use regulations to compensation by state or local governments. These statutes would have required state, city, county, and metropolitan districts enforcing land use regulations to either reimburse landowners who had acquired their property prior to the land use regulations being enacted for fair market value lost, or to waive enforcement, a feature commonly called "pay-or-waive." The initiatives would have applied to regulations such as requirements that any portion of a property remain in its natural state, or restrictions on logging or vegetation removal. The initiatives would also have applied to restrictions on the parcelization or subdivision of property for housing or other development.

At the time that M37 was considered by the electorate, the Oregon constitution already required the government to pay owners "just compensation" when condemning private property or taking property by other action, including laws precluding all substantial beneficial or economically viable use. Similarly, Washington's constitution already required state and local governments to pay an owner of private property just compensation before taking or damaging private property for a public use, and in general, prohibited government from taking private property for public use. Measure 37 included exceptions for regulations that restricted "activities commonly and historically recognized as public nuisances under common law" related to the protection of public health and safety, compliance with federal laws, and restrictions on using property for "selling pornography or performing nude dancing." Yet arguments against M37 and I933 cited vague language and loopholes these acts created in already established laws. The wording establishing pay-or-waive modified the definition of the term "damage" while also describing the scope of damage requiring compensation in broad terms. The language in these sections of M37 and I933 demonstrates to what extent the definition of "damage" would have been extended:

> M37: (1) If a public entity enacts or enforces a new land use regulation or enforces a land use regulation enacted prior to the effective date of this amendment that restricts the use of private real property or any interest therein and has the effect of reducing the fair market value of the property, or any interest therein, then the owner of the property shall be paid just compensation…(B) "Land use regulation" shall include: (i) Any statute regulating the use of land or any interest therein; (ii) Administrative rules and goals of the Land Conservation and Development Commission; (iii) Local government comprehensive plans, zoning ordinances, land division ordinances, and transportation ordinances; (iv) Metropolitan service district regional framework plans, functional plans, planning goals and objectives; and (v) Statutes and administrative rules regulating farming and forest practices.

I933: …means to prohibit or restrict the use of private property to obtain benefit to the public, the cost of which in all fairness and justice should be borne by the public as a whole, and includes, but is not limited to: (i) Prohibiting or restricting any use or size, scope, or intensity of any use legally existing or permitted as of January 1, 1996…(v) Requiring a portion of property to be left in its natural state or without beneficial use to its owner, unless necessary to prevent immediate harm human health and safety; or (vi) Prohibiting maintenance or removal of trees or vegetation.

Measure 37 and I933 did not establish a funding mechanism to compensate landowners.

Measure 37 and I933 did not establish a funding mechanism to compensate landowners nor did they identify clear parameters defining how the value of the damage would be determined. Without the ability to compensate landowners, it was anticipated that most government entities would waive the land use policies that motivated claims. However, there were cases in which claimants were compensated under M37. For example, as the first-ever M37-induced compensation payment, the city of Prineville in Crook County paid the Grover Palin family $180,000 (4 percent of the city's general fund) in compensation for prohibiting building construction on a parcel of undeveloped rim rock overlooking the city (Associated Press 2007). Under Oregon's M37, if the government was unable to compensate a claimant within 2 years of the claim, the law allowed the claimant to use the property under only the regulations in place at the time the property was purchased. Initiative 933, which would have added new sections to Chapter 64.40 (Property rights—damages from governmental actions) and Chapter 36.70A (Growth management—planning by selected counties and cities) of the revised code of Washington, would only have allowed landowners to seek compensation for regulations adopted since January 1, 1996.

Measure 37, if enacted, was estimated to require state administrative expenditures of between $18 million and $44 million per year to respond to claims for compensation (Oregon Secretary of State 2004a). Additionally, local government administrative expenditures expected for M37 claims were estimated at between $46 million and $300 million per year. It was estimated that I933 would cost state agencies slightly more than $2 billion over 6 years for compensation to property owners and administrative costs (Washington Secretary of State 2006a). The estimates of costs to cities from I933 ranged from $3.8 to $5.3 billion, and the cost to counties was estimated at around $1.49 to $1.51 billion. By November 2006, when I933 was up for vote in Washington, approximately 3,000 M37 claims had been filed in Oregon requesting more than $6 billion in compensation (Oregon Department of Land Conservation and Development 2008).

Legal Challenges

Both M37 and I933 instigated numerous judicial proceedings. The major court case impacting M37 was *MacPherson v. Department of Administrative Services*, in which a Circuit Court Judge declared M37 unconstitutional. The judge pointed to M37's interference with the power of the legislature to regulate land use in Oregon; the measure's violation of the privileges and immunities clause, which prohibits actions not in the states' interest; and the designation of one class of property owners (i.e., those who bought land prior to regulations) who did not have to obey land use regulations. On the last issue, the judge stated that M37 would create a "special class of citizens," thereby privileging long-time landowners over more recent landowners and neighbors (Lowry and Richardson 2006, Richardson 2006). Additionally, the judge questioned whether a body creating a law and then exempting certain people from following that law amounted to "legislative favoritism" (Lowry and Richardson 2006). Ultimately, the state of Oregon, one of the defendants in the case, appealed the decision to the Oregon Supreme Court. In 2006, the Oregon Supreme Court reversed the decision, ruling that the law was not unconstitutional while noting that the court was not empowered to rule on its efficacy.

In Washington, I933 ended up in court before the measure was even voted on, with the opposition challenging the wording to be used on the ballot. The League of Women Voters, the Washington Association of Cities, and the Washington Audubon Society challenged the ballot title in Thurston County Superior Court on the grounds that the wording did not accurately reflect changes the initiative would implement. The title stated that the initiative "would require compensation when any government regulation damages the use or value of private property." Opponents complained that the title deceived voters by omitting major pieces of information. Opponents proposed the alternative title, "This measure would require government studies before adopting restrictions on property use, exempt or pay property owners who object to certain zoning, environmental and other laws, and prevent regulations prohibiting previously existing uses." In this case, the presiding judge did not agree that the ballot title was misleading and made only minor changes to the original wording, and this decision was final and immune from appeal.

M37 and I933 Opposition

The M37 opposition included a number of farm bureaus, nonprofit environmental organizations, city mayors, and estate vineyards (Oregon Secretary of State 2004b). Opposition also included Governor Ted Kulongoski (D) and former Governor Victor Atiyeh (R), the American Institute of Architects, Oregon Agricultural

Alliance, Oregon Association for Retired Citizens, League of Women Voters, 1,000 friends of Oregon, American Farmland Trust, American Cancer Society, American Heart Association, and the American Lung Association (Oregon Secretary of State 2004b). The opposition argued the legislation would increase bureaucracy and that since a large portion of a property's value is created by legislation (laws providing for public roads, sewers, electrical lines, parks, and other infrastructure), it was unreasonable to require the government to compensate property owners for any additional legislation that might restrict property use in the name of a public good. They also noted the potential environmental impact of waived measures, the questionable legality, the expected financial burden to taxpayers, the absence of a stated procedure for valuing property losses, and the lack of a notice requirement to neighbors. The environmental impact of waived measures was a particular concern, as many worried about the loss of farmland, forest land, and open space that would result from M37 if keystone land use regulations were waived for M37 claimants. Protecting these lands was among the primary objectives of Oregon's land use planning program from the outset.

Although M37 opponents were better funded than its proponents, they failed to win an electoral majority. Many M37 opponents later criticized the opposition strategy as having been too cerebral. The pro-M37 campaign focused on emotional pleas and personal stories, whereas the anti-M37 coalition focused on general practicalities (e.g., box 1). Opposition to I933 in Washington adopted a different approach. Arguments against I933 raised more specific concerns and potential impacts, such as habitat fragmentation, opening up neighborhoods to indiscriminate development, moving land use decisions out of communities into courtrooms, dismantling zoning laws, the cost to taxpayers from lawsuits, and loss of quality of life and amenities. Specific examples were provided. For example, the opposition pointed out that development would result in more roads, which in turn would result in increased runoff, further undermining the health of Puget Sound. Some credit the anti-I933 coalition's success to lessons learned from the M37 campaign in Oregon. Others credit reaching out to a broad electorate, including the urban population, while M37 failed to engage urban voters.

Opposition to I933 (e.g., box 2) was composed of environmental nonprofits (e.g., The Nature Conservancy, The National Wildlife Federation), all six of Washington's living governors, both of the state's U.S. senators, several state representatives (including Fred Jarrett [R] and Sam Hunt [D]), the Greater Seattle Chamber of Commerce, neighborhood associations and the Washington Association of Churches, various unions (United Farm Workers, United Food and Commercial Workers, etc.), the League of Women Voters, the Affiliated Tribes of Northwest

**Box 1: Example Measure 37 opposition statement
(Oregon Secretary of State 2004b)**

- As farmers and ranchers, we are the true stewards of the land and this measure will not benefit agriculture's land-use protections. Measure 37 is all about destroying wise land-use planning, and not true compensation for property rights takings. Oregon taxpayers do not have, and will not have the financial resources to fund this measure.

- Like farmers throughout Oregon, Jefferson and Grant County farmers rely on stable agricultural zones to continue to thrive and flourish. The irrigated lands have good soils, valuable water rights, and farm use taxation. If measure 37 passes, farmland owners will have a different set of land-use regulations, depending upon their or their ancestors date of purchase. This will result in total chaos, numerous conflicts, and endless litigation. This is exactly what measure 37 proposes. Creating a reckless, wasteful policy resulting in lawyers being the true beneficiaries, not the citizens of Oregon.

- Recently, Madras residents were opposed to a feedlot 1.5 miles away in an agricultural zone. If measure 37 passes, a feedlot could be next door. Just as farmers expect zones free of urban sprawl and conflicts, suburban homeowners should demand the continuation of residential zones free from agricultural and industrial hazards and nuisances. Passage of measure 37 would jeopardize the safeguards of zoning.

- The sum total of every property owner's desires is more than society can afford. To allow a house on any hill or every parcel would quickly exhaust all public dollars for roads, mail service, school busing, fire protection, law enforcement, and utilities. The vast rangeland areas of Jefferson and Grant Counties should remain working ranches!

- The compensation clause will not apply to any federal rules and/or regulations or health and safety issues.

—Jefferson and Grant County Farm Bureau

Box 2: Initiative 933 opposition statement
(Washington Secretary of State 2006a)

A POORLY WRITTEN, LOOPHOLE-RIDDEN INITIATIVE THAT LEAVES HUNDREDS OF QUESTIONS UNANSWERED

Initiative 933 is deceptive and misleading. It provides no protection from eminent domain abuses. Instead, the special interests behind I-933 crafted loopholes that force Washington taxpayers to pay billions to a small group of property owners, or force communities to waive safeguards against irresponsible development.

WHO BENEFITS FROM I-933'S LOOPHOLES?

Here is an example of how the loopholes work. If laws prevent a property owner from expanding a strip mall in a neighborhood or building a subdivision on farmland, I-933 would force the community into a no-win choice—either waive the law or have taxpayers pay the property owner for not being able to build.

How will governments decide which laws to waive and who taxpayers pay? One thing is certain: I-933 is so poorly written it will generate endless lawsuits. Special interests will hire the best lawyers and win out over communities. The lawyers' fees and administration alone will cost taxpayers millions.

Don't be fooled—irresponsible development hurts farming. Hundreds of family farmers oppose I-933.

WHY WILL I-933 COST TAXPAYERS SO MUCH?
AND WHERE WILL THE MONEY COME FROM?

In Oregon, a similar law generated almost $4 billion in claims against taxpayers. I-933 could cost each Washington taxpayer thousands yearly in additional taxes or lost services.

HOW WILL I-933 HARM SAFEGAURDS FOR
OUR COMMUNITIES?

Communities have worked hard to protect their quality of life, but I-933 applies retroactively to laws going back at least 10 years! This would force communities to waive hundreds of existing safeguards we have depended on to protect neighborhoods and farmland, and prevent water pollution, traffic, and over-development.

I-933 is a costly assortment of loopholes, lawsuits, and special deals. Please vote *no*!

Indians, the American Lung Association of Washington, and a number of prominent individuals, such as Bill Gates (Washington Secretary of State 2006a). Many organizations that had supported initiatives similar to I933 in the past were neutral. The Washington Association of Realtors voiced concerns about tax increases, litigation, and regulatory confusion; many worried the initiative would bring instability to the real estate market. Organizations such as the Master Builders Association of King and Snohomish Counties, which supports property rights, did not oppose I933 outright, yet they did voice concerns that the poorly drafted initiative could, "create as many problems as it solves" (Pryne 2006). Other neutral parties included major Washington timberland owners Simpson Timber, Plum Creek, and Longview Fibre—although these landowners were among the top 10 donors to Referendum 48 (a previous landowner rights ballot measure in Washington) in 1995 (Pryne 2006).

M37 and I933 Support

The supporters of M37 included several state senators and representatives, some timber- industry-related organizations (e.g., Seneca Sawmill Company, Freres Lumber Co., Inc.), and various political action committees (PAC) (e.g., Family Farm Preservation, Oregon Citizens for a Sound Economy) (Oregon Secretary of State 2004c). Although the timber companies and real estate developers in Washington remained neutral toward I933, in Oregon these entities were some of the most prominent supporters and primary funders of M37 (Harden 2005). Seneca Jones Timber Co. was the largest single donor to the M37 campaign. Although many agriculturally minded PACs supported M37, state financial records show that small family farmers contributed very little to the Family Farm Preservation PAC that bankrolled Measure 37; most of the money came from timber companies and real estate interests (Harden 2005).

Dorothy English became the face of the M37 campaign.

Dorothy English, an elderly woman who identified herself as a Democrat, became the face of the M37 campaign. Owing to Oregon forest land zoning, English's land could not be subdivided. Mrs. English claimed that she had always intended to subdivide her land into parcels that could be evenly allocated to her children. English's story was repeated on radio ads throughout the state in the months leading up to election day (Harden 2005) (e.g., box 3). Other personal stories also were brought to the public's attention, particularly those involving "lots of record," individual parcels usually surrounded by properties large enough to warrant exclusive farm use zones but too small to generate enough farm produce to meet an agricultural revenue test required for the owner to build a house. Proponents of M37 also appealed to rural voters by claiming that they were disproportionally hindered by Oregon's land use regulations system (Oregon Secretary of State 2004c).

**Box 3: Example Measure 37 supporting statement
(Oregon Secretary of State 2004c)**

I am a Chief Petitioner for Ballot Measure 37. Some say I am the poster child for Ballot Measure 37. My husband and I purchased our property in 1953. It was our dream to someday divide the property, give some of it to our children and grandchildren, and sell [what] remained for our retirement. We have always paid our taxes, and never been on any type of tax deferral. Nevertheless, Multnomah County zoned our property as commercial forest land even though there isn't a commercial timber operation anywhere near our property. What's more, Multnomah County knows our property is mis-zoned, but refuses to do anything about it. Oregon's land use planning system is supposed to be balanced and fair. It is neither. Multnomah County has made it perfectly clear to me, and many other property owners, that the county intends to be neither balanced nor fair. Governor Kulongoski told Multnomah County that he sympathized with my problem and asked the County to work with me to help resolve my case. But the County refused to help. Multnomah County Chairwoman Diane Linn even personally asked the Governor to veto a bill that would have restored some of the rights my husband and I had when we first purchased the property—that is how unfair Multnomah County has been. Opponents of Ballot Measure 37 are trying to scare the voters into opposing this measure. Please do not believe their scare tactics. Ballot Measure 37 will help senior citizens like myself recover what has been stolen from us. Oregon's land use planning system is in need of repair. Our elected leaders, community leaders, and newspapers, are unwilling to support the necessary changes. It's time for Oregonians to do the work ourselves. It is time we say "no" to the scare tactics and restore fairness and balance to the system. Thank you for taking the time to read my comments. Please vote yes on Ballot Measure 37.

—Dorothy English

The Washington State Farm Bureau led the I933 campaign and employed complaints about urbanites, particularly Seattle-area residents in King County (67 percent of King County residents voted against I933). Proponents painted a picture of city dwellers setting the legislative obstacles for hard-working farmers (e.g., box 4). Supporters also bemoaned how stringent land use regulation had gotten in the state, with talk of eminent domain or eminent domain reform (although I933 had no eminent domain provisions). Other groups, such as the Washington Association of Realtors and other traditional Washington State Farm Bureau allies, were deeply divided on I933 (Pryne 2006b). Skagit County's agricultural community was especially divided on whether or not to support I933 (Clever 2006). The farming community was at odds with those in the livestock and dairy industry who had concerns over streamside buffer regulations for the protection of salmon (*Oncorhynchus* spp.*)*, while others in agriculture shared a concern about maintaining provisions that helped to protect farmland from development. A considerable portion of the financial support for I933 came from out-of-state contributors, with the largest portion coming from Howard Rich's 501(c)(3) Chicago-based Americans for Limited Government (Lowery and Richardson 2006). Other supporters included Bainbridge Citizens United, Spokane Pro-America, the Building Industry Association of Washington, and the Washington Cattleman's Association. A number of county farm bureaus lent support and provided funding to promote passage of I933.

Methods

Empirical Approach

The general approach adopted in this study follows that of Kline and Armstrong (2001), which followed on Deacon and Shapiro (1975). Ordinary least squares (OLS) regression was used to examine M37 and I933 voting relative to socioeconomic, demographic, and landscape characteristics. Lacking individual voting observations, the unit of analysis we adopted was the county using county-level voting results obtained from secretary of state offices in both states (Oregon Secretary of State, n.d.; Washington Secretary of State 2006b). Following regression methods reported in Kline and Armstrong (2001), the dependent variable used in our models is the natural log of the percentage of votes "yes" (yes_i) divided by the percentage of votes "no," all for county i:

$$\text{Logit } (yes_i) = \ln [P(yes_i) \div (1 - P(yes_i))] .$$

Known as a logit transformation, the specification bounds the dependent variable between zero and 1.

**Box 4: Initiative 933 supporting statement
(Washington Secretary of State 2006a)**

Initiative 933, the Property Fairness Act, will restore balance between government's power to regulate and the people's constitutional right to own and use private property.

IT'S FAIR: PROTECTING THE USE OF PRIVATE PROPERTY PROTECTS OUR JOBS, RETIREMENTS AND PUBLIC SERVICES

In the past 10 years, excessive government regulations have violated our rights and made it difficult for farmers and other property owners to use their property in reasonable ways.

For most of us, our homes are our greatest investment. Government should not be able to change the rules and strip us of the use or value of our private property. I-933 protects our jobs, our economy and our retirement plans that depend on reasonable use of private property.

IT'S FAIR: I-933 REQUIRES GOVERNMENT TO CONSIDER COSTS AND RESPECT PROPERTY OWNERS' RIGHTS

Too often, government adopts regulations without fully understanding the impact on the people it represents. I-933 will require government to identify the likely impact on property owners and pursue voluntary, cooperative efforts to achieve environmental goals before adopting new regulations.

IT'S FAIR: I-933 RETURNS RESPONSIBILITY FOR LAND-USE PLANNING TO LOCAL GOVERNMENT AND CITIZENS

Instead of accepting top-down mandates from unelected state officials, local government will be required to assess the impact of its actions on local property owners, thus giving citizens more say in local land-use decisions, and holding local officials accountable for their actions. Agencies can choose whether to compensate property owners or avoid damaging the use and value of private property. But the main point of I-933 is to have government avoid damaging property in the first place.

IT'S FAIR: I-933 REQUIRES GOVERNMENT TO RESPECT OUR RIGHTS AND FOLLOW THE CONSTITUTION

Washington's state constitution says, "No private property shall be taken or damaged...without just compensation." I-933 will force government to respect our rights and follow the constitution.

Explanatory Variables

Using previous literature as guidance, we considered a number of explanatory variables hypothesized as useful predictors of voting patterns for initiatives involving land use regulation in Oregon and Washington (table 2-1). Previous studies have shown that socioeconomic characteristics often correspond to voting patterns on initiatives related to conservation, open space, and property rights. Household income, education, and partisan political affiliation were considered as variables because past research has found that these characteristics correspond positively to environmental values (Kline 2006, Press 2003). Partisan affiliation, in particular, has shown strong correlations to support for environmental measures (Jones and Dunlap 1992, Press 2003). For Oregon, the percentage of the county's electorate in November 2004 registered as Democrats was used to indicate political affiliation. Washington's blanket primary system made it difficult to determine party affiliation in that state. Lacking political party registration figures for Washington, we used the percentage of votes by county for Kerry/Edwards in the 2004 general election as a proxy for Washington voter political affiliation. Also considered as a predictor of land use referendum voting behavior was the county's status as a metropolitan area as defined in the 2003 rural-urban continuum codes (Economic Research Service 2003). Previous research has shown correspondence between urban populations and environmental protection behavior (Jones and Dunlap 1992). The percentage of adult population that was native Oregonian was included in the models, consistent with Kline and Armstrong (2001). Census reports indicate that migration to Oregon and Washington tends to bring young residents who cluster around urban areas and who are often more educated than the state's existing residents, especially in Oregon (Vaidya 2001). These inmigrants often have socioeconomic characteristics that are linked to increased concern for the environment.

Both agriculture and forestry employment were expected to be correlated with voting behavior. Forest sector employment, as a percentage of total employment, was found to be a useful explanatory variable in Kline and Armstrong (2001). Both the forestry sector and forest landowners would have been affected by M37 and I933 owing to existing legislation in both states that related to forest practices and forest land use. Similarly, the agriculture sector and landowners were expected to be affected by M37 and I933 through both the potential for increased residential development, which might reduce the agricultural land available and allowed management practices (e.g., field burning), and a greater opportunity for individual landowners to profit from the sale of agriculture land for development. Pro-M37

Socioeconomic characteristics often correspond to voting patterns on initiatives related to conservation.

Table 2-1—Definitions and sources of explanatory variables tested in the empirical model

Variable	Definition	Source
Population density	People per square mile of land area, 2005	USDC Census Bureau 2006a, 2006b
Population change	Numeric change in population, 2000 to 2005	USDC Census Bureau 2006a, 2006b
Percentage population	Percentage change in population, 2000 to 2005	USDC Census Bureau 2006a, 2006b
Housing change	Numeric change in housing units, 2000 to 2005	USDC Census Bureau 2006c, 2006d
Percentage housing increase[a]	Percentage change in housing units, 2000 to 2005	USDC Census Bureau 2006c, 2006d
Household income[a]	Median household income in 2005	USDC Census Bureau 2008
College educated[a]	Percentage of individuals in county age 25 years or older with a 4-year college degree or higher in 2000	USDC Census Bureau 2003a, 2003b
Forest employment[a]	Percentage of workers employed in forestry-related sectors, 2004	Minnesota IMPLAN Group, n.d.
Agricultural employment[a]	Percentage of workers employed in agriculture-related sectors, 2004	Minnesota IMPLAN Group, n.d.
Metropolitan area[a]	Counties classified as metropolitan areas in the rural-urban continuum codes	Economic Research Service 2003
Counties adjacent to metropolitan area	Counties classified as nonmetropolitan areas but located adjacent to a metropolitan area	Economic Research Service 2003
Percentage private land[a]	Percentage of county land area in private ownership	Theobald 2007
Median age	Median age of the population in 2000	USDC Census Bureau 2003a, 2003b
Percentage Democratic[a]	In Oregon, percentage of electorate registered as Democrats in November 2004. In Washington, percentage of votes for Kerry/Edwards in the 2004 general election	Oregon Secretary of State 2005, Washington Secretary of State 2004
Native born[a]	Percentage of population in 2000 reported to have been born in the state	USDC Census Bureau 2003a, 2003b
Diversity index	Percentage of population reporting belonging to a minority race or ethnicity	USDC Census Bureau 2002a, 2002b

[a] Variable included in final model.

and 1933 coalitions had argued that land use regulations such as the Growth Management Act (GMA) (Washington) and Senate Bill 100 (Oregon) had hurt farmers by lowering farm land values. In this study, the percentage of the workforce in agricultural employment was used as a measure of the importance of the agriculture sector to local communities.

Finally, several variables characterizing the physical landscape of counties were also considered. Population density and change in density have been found to correlate with increased public support for preserving local open space (Kline 2006). Housing development and the percentage and nominal increase in housing units were also considered to characterize local development. Lastly, the limited amount of available private land is often mentioned as a factor in western land use issues, and Washington and Oregon both have extensive areas of publicly owned land. To account for the limited land base available for private development, we calculated the percentage of the county in private land using a spatial database of public and privately owned land (Theobald 2007) and the census-reported land area of each county.

Estimated Models

Three OLS models were estimated: individual models constructed for both Oregon and Washington and one combined model that used observations pooled from both states. With the exception of a dummy variable to identify observations from Washington in the combined model, the same explanatory variables were used in all three models. The individual state models provide insight into the voting patterns for land use planning referenda that we were able to discern for each state. The combined model capitalizes on the greater number of observations pooled from both states to provide general insight into voter behavior regarding land use planning referenda generally. As heteroscedasticity can be common in voting behavior models, we also estimated models using weighted least squares (WLS). However, as the WLS models did little to improve the standard errors on the coefficients and as the interpretation of results did not differ between the OLS and WLS models, we report only models estimated via the more parsimonious OLS regression.

Results

In Oregon, the electorate voted 1,054,589 to 685,079 to pass M37. Only in Benton County did the electorate vote against measure 37 (fig. 2-1). Benton County ranks as Oregon's most-educated populace, with 40 percent of the electorate registered as Democrats, and had experienced one of the highest housing growth rates in the state. Although M37 won a majority of voters in Multnomah County, which includes Oregon's largest city, Portland, a strong contingent of individuals there voted "no." The strongest support for M37 existed in the relatively rural Counties of Baker, Coos, Douglas, Grant, Harney, Josephine, Klamath, Lake, and Morrow.

In Washington, voters turned down I933—1,199,679 to 839,992—with 59 percent voting against it. The popularity of I933 was evident in places like rapidly developing Yakima Valley and the Vancouver metro area. Conversely, voters along the Interstate-5 corridor living predominantly in urban communities voted overwhelmingly against the initiative (fig. 2-2). Voters in Skagit County voted most strongly against I933 with 70 percent of county residents voting "no," while Ferry County voters were nearly the opposite with 62 percent voting "yes." Skagit County lies at the upper end of the spectrum of median income while lying in the midrange for percentage holding a bachelor's degree; both forestry and agricultural employment rates were low. Ferry County's median household income and percentage

The popularity of I933 was evident in places like rapidly developing Yakima Valley and the Vancouver metro area.

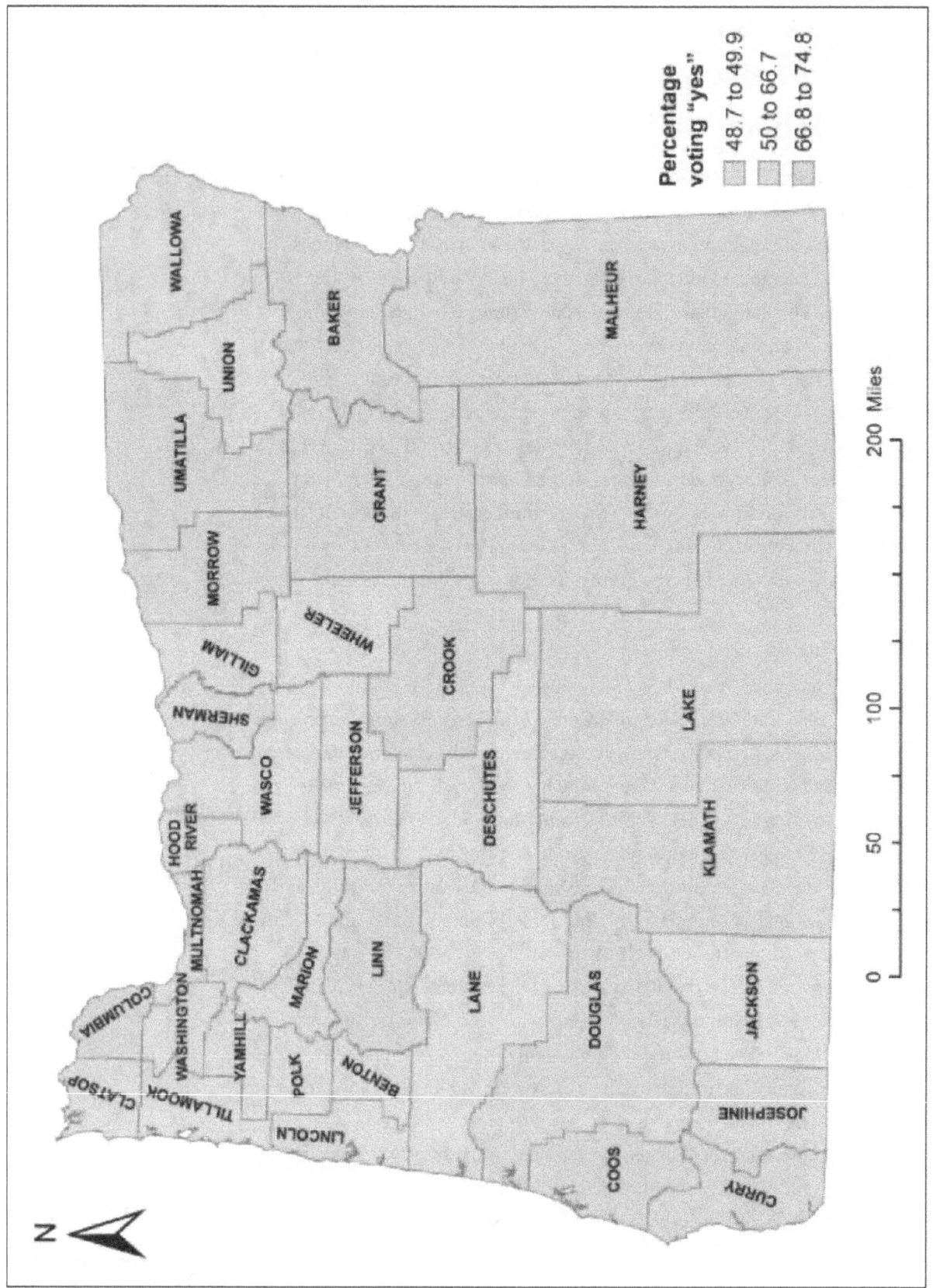

Figure 2-1—County-level voting pattern for Oregon's Measure 37.

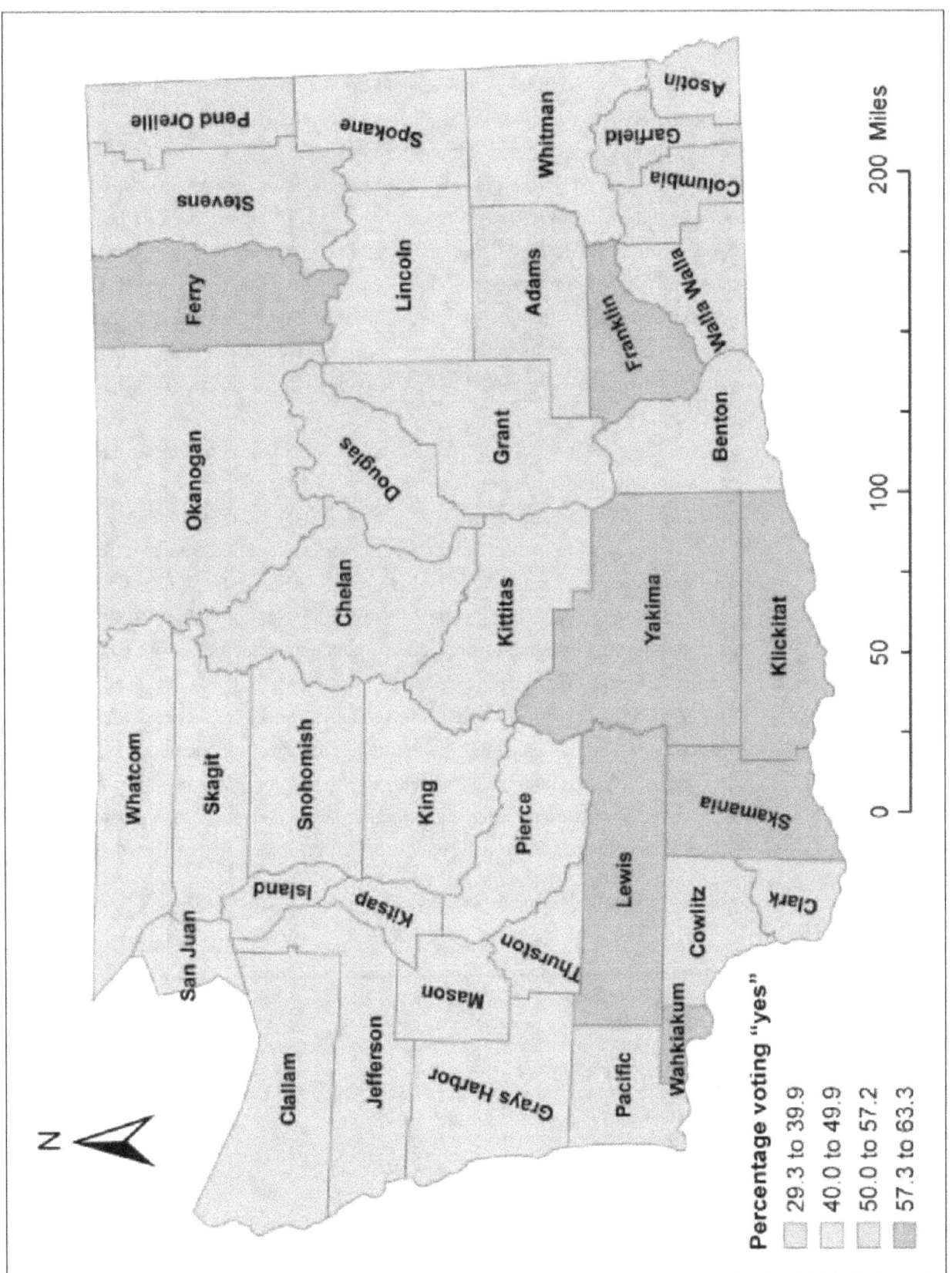

Figure 2-2—County-level voting pattern for Washington's Initiative 933.

Percentage voting "yes"

29.3 to 39.9
40.0 to 49.9
50.0 to 57.2
57.3 to 63.3

holding at least a bachelor's degree was less than the statewide average. Forestry employment was high in Ferry County relative to the statewide pattern.

Collectively, the independent variables in the model of voting behavior for Oregon's M37 were statistically significant predictors of the likelihood of voting "yes" with an F-statistic of 10.90 and an adjusted R^2 of 0.72 (table 2-2). Voting behavior toward M37 is largely explained by education level, political party affiliation, and the percentage of increase in housing units experienced in the county between 2000 and 2005. All else being equal, voters were less likely to vote "yes" on M37 as (1) the percentage of the population with college degrees increased, (2) as Democratic party political affiliation increased, or (3) the recent percentage increase in housing units in the county became greater. Individually, the remaining variables included in the model had no statistically significant influence on the likelihood of voting "yes."

Similarly, the independent variables in the Washington model were found to be statistically significant predictors of the likelihood of voting "yes" with an adjusted R^2 of 0.68 and an F-statistic of 6.76 (table 2-3). Household income, level of education, employment in the forestry sector, and the percentage of electorate voting Democratic were found to be individually statistically significant predictors of voting "yes." All else being equal, the probability of voting "yes" declined as education level, household income, and percentage of electorate voting Democratic increased. Employment in the forestry sector increased the likelihood of voting "yes" on I933, all else being equal. The remaining variables were not found independently to be statistically significant predictors of voting behavior.

The combined model resulting in an adjusted R^2 of 0.80 and an F-statistic of 31.07 (table 2-4). All else being equal, higher household incomes, a greater percentage of the electorate with college education, and Democratic Party affiliation were

Table 2-2—County-level model of Oregon voting behavior for Measure 37[a]

	Coefficient	T-statistic	P-value
Intercept	2.34112	6.60	0.000
Household income	0.00001	0.80	0.432
College educated	-0.02653	-5.03	0.000
Percentage Democratic	-3.18646	-4.83	0.000
Percentage housing increase	-1.58638	-1.89	0.070
Forest employment	2.59553	0.88	0.385
Agricultural employment	-0.61566	-1.32	0.200
Metropolitan area	0.07724	0.75	0.462
Native born	-0.00508	-1.09	0.286
Percentage private land	0.00914	0.05	0.960

Adj R^2 = 0.72, F = 10.90, P-value <0.001.
[a] Dependent variable: likelihood of voting "yes."

Table 2-3—County-level model of Washington voting behavior for Initiative 933[a]

	Coefficient	T-statistic	P-value
Intercept	1.54704	2.89	0.007
Household income	-0.00002	-2.10	0.045
College educated	-0.01444	-1.92	0.065
Percentage Democratic	-1.28835	-1.77	0.087
Percentage housing increase	1.00560	0.95	0.348
Forest employment	4.82945	2.26	0.032
Agricultural employment	0.72646	0.76	0.456
Metropolitan area	0.17688	1.52	0.139
Native born	-0.00272	-0.51	0.612
Percentage private land	0.02724	0.15	0.881

Adj R^2 = 0.68, F = 6.76, P-value <0.001.
[a] Dependent variable: likelihood of voting "yes."

Table 2-4—County-level model of Oregon and Washington voting behavior for measures to limit the power of land use planning laws [a]

	Coefficient	T-statistic	P-value
Intercept	2.06607	7.29	0.000
Household income	-0.00001	-1.68	0.097
College educated	-0.01932	-4.36	0.000
Percentage Democratic	-1.74388	-4.02	0.000
Percentage housing increase	0.37878	0.57	0.572
Forest employment	3.54217	2.28	0.026
Agricultural employment	0.12651	0.27	0.788
Metropolitan area	0.09055	1.19	0.237
Native born	-0.00282	-0.82	0.418
Percentage private land	0.02793	0.24	0.812
Washington counties	-0.49662	-8.11	0.000

Adj R^2 = 0.80, F = 31.07, P-value <0.001.
[a] Dependent variable: likelihood of voting "yes."

negatively correlated with the likelihood of voting "yes" on a measure to limit land use planning. Conversely, all else being equal, forestry employment was positively correlated with the likelihood of voting "yes." Measure I933 was defeated in Washington and the dummy variable included to indicate Washington observations was found to have a statistically significant negative effect, indicating Washingtonians were less likely to vote "yes" on the land use planning measure they considered. We are unable to discern from the results of this study if the lesser likelihood of voting "yes" for Washingtonians relates to voters having a different set of information (e.g., from the supporting and opposing arguments) than those in Oregon, a different view by the populace of the ballot measure, a predisposition to vote against measures limiting land use planning, or some other factor.

Voter behavior for M37 and I933 was consistent with past studies suggesting a relationship between socioeconomic characteristics and voter support.

Discussion

In general, voter behavior for M37 and I933 was consistent with past studies suggesting a relationship between socioeconomic characteristics and voter support for environmental-related referenda (e.g., Jones and Dunlap 1992, Kline and Armstrong 2001, Salka 2003). In Oregon, the likelihood of voting "yes" on M37 decreased as counties contained more college-educated individuals, a higher percentage of Democrats, and had experienced greater percentage increases in the number of housing units in recent years. Employment in the forestry and agriculture sectors, status as a metropolitan area, the percentage of residents who were native Oregonians, and the percentage of the county land base in private ownership individually had no significant influence on the probability of voting "yes."

Many individuals would state that M37 passed because it reflected the will of the voters. Others would argue that the measure passed because of a number of other factors unrelated to the aim of the measure itself: an unclear ballot title, an incomplete understanding among voters of the legislative and fiscal effects of the measure, the ballot initiative system, and a poorly strategized marketing campaign by the anti-M37 coalition. Oregonians in Action utilized an effective marketing/public relations strategy, which focused on a loss of "rights" while also claiming that agricultural land had lost value owing to land use regulations. In addition, the ballot summary of M37 highlighted the monetary compensation rather than the granting of land use waivers. The anti-M37 coalition seems to have failed in engaging urban voters by creating commercials that focused more on farmers and their concerns rather than on the value of maintaining open space to the broader public. Initiative 933 opponents, on the other hand, actively engaged urban voters through their marketing program.

In Washington state, the probability of voting "yes" on I933 was found to be lower in counties with higher household incomes, higher levels of college education, and a greater percentage of Democrats. The probability of voting "yes" on I933 increased with the percentage of the county workforce employed by the forestry sector. Employment in the agriculture sector, metropolitan area status, recent changes in the number of housing units, the extent of the population being native Washingtonians, and the percentage of the county in private land were not found to have statistically significant influence individually on probability of voting "yes." The lack of influence of living in a metropolitan area is particularly interesting given the anti-I933 emphasis on courting metropolitan voters.

Although the results of the models indicate similarity in the factors influencing voting patterns and relative similarities between the two states, M37 passed while I933 did not. Some have pointed to the time lapse between the two votes as one explanation for the different outcomes. Washington's I933 was presented to voters 2 years after M37 was passed in Oregon, over which time Washington voters had witnessed the administrative and financial difficulties experienced in Oregon in the aftermath of M37. Some arguments in opposition to I933 even cited the situation in Oregon as one reason to oppose I933. In this study, we were unable to characterize in the Washington model the extent to which the Oregon experience with M37 influenced voter behavior for individual Washington counties. In future studies of voter behavior on natural resource-related referenda, it may be useful to consider what effect outcomes from ballot measures in one state may have on later voting outcomes for similar measures in other states.

The Pacific Northwest has had a strong history of land use regulation. In Oregon, this regulation dates back to the early 1970s, with Senate Bill 100 establishing Oregon's Land Conservation and Development Commission and Portland's 1972 Downtown Plan establishing stringent land use guidelines. Since that time, Oregon has been recognized nationally for its progressive incorporation of land use planning at state and local levels. The citizenry's willingness to enact such measures seems to indicate the high priority they place on protecting agricultural, forest, and natural resource lands. Although not as far reaching, a similar legacy exists for Washington. The GMA, enacted in 1990, requires state and local governments to identify and protect critical areas and natural resource lands as well as to designate urban-growth areas and boundaries aimed at accommodating the majority of projected population increases.

Oregon and Washington's populace are generally considered to have strong environmental consciousness, a factor that would be expected to influence voting outcomes. However, the passage of M37 is an indication that these environmental values are not cast in stone, but rather oscillate with shifting priorities and concerns among the citizenry and the persistent tension between upholding private property rights and regulating private use of land. In 1992, an Oregon Values and Beliefs Survey was launched, and a 2002 report documented changes in values between 1992 and 2002 (DHMCOR, n.d.). Although natural beauty, environmental quality, and a small town feel were reasons cited for why Oregonians like their communities, the priority rankings of Oregonians for such things as clean drinking water, parks and recreation, natural resources management, environmental regulation, and mass transit decreased between 1992 and 2002 relative to other items. When asked, "Is it likely/desirable that over the next 10 years environmental protection will become more important than economic growth?" responses indicating "likely" and "desirable" decreased (DHMCOR, n.d.). A more thorough examination of environmentally conscious behavior of Oregonians could be helpful in identifying shifts in values and priorities and may help explain voter behavior over time.

Over the last 10 years, Oregon voters have been somewhat erratic in voting behavior toward land use planning legislation. Measures 65 (1998) and 2 (2000), which both sought to restrict the legislature's ability to regulate land use, failed. However, Measure 7 (2000), an initiative similar to M37, was approved by voters, before it was struck down by the Oregon Supreme Court. Post-M37, in 2006, Oregon voters passed Measure 39, which attempted to exempt forests, farmlands, and open spaces from M37 (Measure 39 was ultimately also struck down by the Oregon Supreme Court). Also in 2006, results of a poll of 405 registered Oregon voters who voted in the 2004 November election including M37 indicated that were it to be voted on again, M37 would not pass (Greenberg, Quinlan, and Rosner 2006). And finally, in 2007, Measure 49 was passed by 62 percent. There seem to be many conflicting values and priorities at play, as well as an issue of perception and how people understand concepts. Harden (2005) noted the paradox of a citizenry with higher-than-average environmental values passing measures to limit land use planning, stating, "(M37) illustrates a nationwide paradox in public opinion: although voters tend to favor protection of farmland and open space, they vote down these protections if they perceive them as restrictions on personal rights." Further research that goes beyond wording and focuses on the description of rights and personal freedoms on ballot measure descriptions could prove useful.

Initiative 933, on the other hand, was inspired by both M37 and a similar measure that reached the Washington ballot in 1995, Referendum 48 (R48). Referendum 48 would have required compensation for landowners for regulations imposed for "public benefit" that reduced property values, but it failed to pass. The Building Industry Association of Washington (BIAW), Washington Association of Realtors, and their national parent organizations were the biggest contributors to the R48 campaign. Yet with I933, those groups only contributed a small amount (Pryne 2006). Many considered it an indication of the industries' acceptance of regulations such as the GMA. In general, Washington's ballot measure history and the socio-economic evidence available paints a picture that predicted likely defeat of I933, whereas the same could surely not have been said of Oregon, particularly in light of the 2000 passage of Measure 7.

Conclusions

In Oregon, counties more likely to oppose M37 had a higher percentage of college-graduates and Democrats, and had experienced faster housing expansion. In addition to the influence of socioeconomic and demographic characteristics, ballot wording and a strong marketing campaign by the pro-M37 coalition are touted as reasons for passage of M37. Washington's I933 opponents came from counties composed of more educated residents earning higher incomes with a large proportion of the populace employed by nonforestry-related sectors and voting Democratic in 2004.

The results of the combined model of voting on M37 and I933 largely mirrored the results for the state-specific models. Increasing percentages of the populace with college-degrees, higher household incomes, and Democratic party political preferences, all lead to decreased likelihood of supporting the referenda. The increased percentage of the workforce employed in the forestry sector increased the likelihood of supporting the referenda, all else being equal. Living in a metropolitan area, the percentage of the population that was native to the state, agriculture employment, and the percentage of the land base in private ownership were found to lack statistically significant impact, independently, on the likelihood of supporting the referenda limiting land use planning.

Voting patterns reflect differing values and priorities regarding the environment and land use planning.

Voting patterns for M37 and I933 seem, in part, to reflect differing values and priorities regarding the environment and land use planning as well as differences in how individuals perceive ballot initiatives. Social scientists have examined changes in the value structures associated with natural resource management (Shindler and Cramer 1999, Steel et al. 1994). Bengston (1994) summarized the usefulness of this inquiry by asserting that managers, policymakers, and scientists can benefit from a better understanding of public values for forests and other natural resources. In this case, the questions put forth could include, Will the environmental and private property values that underlie voting behavior (e.g., on issues like M37 and I933) change with the changing socioeconomic characteristics of Oregon and Washington? What might changing values imply for ecosystem management approaches (or tools) and future voting outcomes? Measure 37 and historical patterns of voting for land use referenda show that there is a great deal of back and forth regarding land use legislation in Oregon. County socioeconomic changes and major demographic changes imply that some major changes on the electoral landscape are arriving, although how exactly these changes will influence land use legislation and protection of the environment and natural resources are difficult to predict.

References

Associated Press. 2007. Prineville makes Oregon's first Measure 37 payment. http://blog.oregonlive.com/breakingnews/2007/09/prineville_makes_oregons_first.html. (January 16, 2009).

Bengston, D.N. 1994. Changing forest values and ecosystem management. Society and Natural Resources. 7: 515–533.

Clever, D. 2006. County farmers split on I-933. Skagit Valley Herald. http://pioneer. olivesoftware.com/Repository/ml.asp?Ref=UE1WLzIwMDYvMDcvMjQjQXIw MDEwMQ==&Mode=HTML&Locale=english-skin-custom. (April 9, 2009).

Davis and Hibbitts, Inc.; McCaig Communications & Opinion Research, Inc [DHMCOR]. [N.d.]. Oregon values and beliefs, 2002. http://www.oregonvalues. org/report/index.htm. (April 9, 2009).

Deacon, R.; Shapiro, P. 1975. Private preference for collective goods revealed through voting on referenda. American Economic Review. 65(5): 943–955.

Economic Research Service. 2003. Rural-urban continuum codes. http://www.ers. usda.gov/Data/RuralUrbanContinuumCodes/2003/. (January 16, 2009).

Greenberg, Quinlan, and Rosner. 2006. Oregon statewide poll results: voters have buyer's remorse for Measure 37. www.defendersactionfund.org/newsroom/ oregonpoll.pdf. (April 9, 2009).

Harden, B. 2005. Anti-sprawl laws, property rights collide in Oregon. Washington Post. http://www.washingtonpost.com/ac2/wp-dyn/A58185-2005Feb27?language=printer. (April 9, 2009).

Jones, R.E.; Dunlap, R.E. 1992. The social bases of environmental concern: Have they changed over time? Rural Sociology. 57(1): 28–47.

Kline, J.D. 2006. Public demand for preserving local open space. Society and Natural Resources. 19: 645–659.

Kline, J.D.; Armstrong, C. 2001. Autopsy of a forestry ballot initiative: characterizing voter support for Oregon's Measure 64. Journal of Forestry. 99(5): 20–27.

Lowery, S.; Richardson, D. 2006. The campaign against land use planning. http:// www.newwest.net/index.php/topic/article/the_campaign_to_gut_land_use_ planning/C505/L35/. (April 9, 2009).

Minnesota Implan Group. [N.d.]. IMPLAN Pro county and state data files, 2004. Stillwater, MN.

Oregonians in Action [OIA]. [N.d.]. Background information. http://www.oia.org/ index.php/about-us. (April 9, 2009).

Oregon Department of Land Conservation and Development. 2008. Measure 37—summary of claims. http://www.oregon.gov/LCD/MEASURE37/ summaries_of_claims.shtml. (January 16, 2009).

Oregon Secretary of State. 2004a. Ballot title. http://www.sos.state.or.us/elections/ nov22004/guide/meas/m37_bt.html. (July 20, 2010).

Oregon Secretary of State. 2004b. Measure 37—arguments in opposition. http:// www.sos.state.or.us/elections/nov22004/guide/meas/m37_opp.html. (January 28, 2009).

Oregon Secretary of State. 2004c. Measure 37—arguments in favor. http://www. sos.state.or.us/elections/nov22004/guide/meas/m37_fav.html. (April 9, 2009).

Oregon Secretary of State. 2005. Voter registration by county, 2004. http:// oregonvotes.org/votreg/nov04.pdf. (January 27, 2009).

Oregon Secretary of State. [N.d.]. November 2, 2004, General election abstract of votes state measure No. 37. http://www.sos.state.or.us/elections/nov22004/ abstract/m37.pdf. (April 9, 2009).

Press, D. 2003. Who votes for natural resources in California? Society and Natural Resources. 16(9): 835–846.

Pryne, E. 2006. I-933 finds lukewarm support. The Seattle Times. http:// community.seattletimes.nwsource.com/archive/?date=20060827&slug=proprights27m. (April 9, 2009).

Richardson, D. 2006. Oregon's measure 37 gets its day in court. http://www. newwest.net/index.php/topic/article/5205/C35/L35. (April 9, 2009).

Salka, W.M. 2003. Determinants of countrywide voting behavior on environmental ballot measures: 1990–2000. Rural Sociology. 68(2): 253–277.

Shindler, B.; Cramer, L.A. 1999. Shifting public values for forest management: making sense of wicked problems. Western Journal of Applied Forestry. 14(1): 28–34.

Steel, B.S.; List, P.; Shindler, B. 1994. Conflicting values about federal forests: a comparison of national and Oregon publics. Society and Natural Resources. 7(2): 137–153.

Theobald, D.M. 2007. Protected lands of the continental US (CUS_UPPT_100). Unpublished data. Natural Resource Ecology Lab, Colorado State University, Ft. Collins, CO 80523-1499.

U.S. Department of Commerce, Census Bureau. 2003a. Oregon: 2000 summary social, economic, and housing characteristics. http://www.census.gov/prod/ cen2000/phc-2-39.pdf. (January 27, 2009).

U.S. Department of Commerce, Census Bureau. 2003b. Washington: 2000 summary social, economic, and housing characteristics. http://www.census.gov/prod/cen2000/phc-2-49.pdf. (January 27, 2009).

U.S. Department of Commerce, Census Bureau. 2006a. Table 1: Annual estimates of the population for counties of Washington: April 1, 2000 to July 1, 2005. http://www.census.gov/popest/counties/tables/CO-EST2005-01-53.xls. (January 27, 2009).

U.S. Department of Commerce, Census Bureau. 2006b. Table 1: Annual estimates of the population for counties of Oregon: April 1, 2000 to July 1, 2005. http://www.census.gov/popest/counties/tables/CO-EST2005-01-41.xls. (January 27, 2009).

U.S. Department of Commerce, Census Bureau. 2006c. Annual estimates of housing units for counties in Washington: April 1, 2000 to July 1, 2005. http://www.census.gov/popest/housing/tables/HU-EST2005-04-53.xls. (January 27, 2009).

U.S. Department of Commerce, Census Bureau. 2006d. Annual estimates of housing units for counties in Oregon: April 1, 2000 to July 1, 2005. http://www.census.gov/popest/housing/tables/HU-EST2005-04-41.xls. (January 27, 2009).

U.S. Department of Commerce, Census Bureau. 2008. Model-based small area income and poverty estimates (SAIPE) for school districts, counties, and states [Database]. http://www.census.gov/did/www/saipe/index.html. (January 27, 2009).

Vaidya, K.L. 2001. 2000 Oregon population survey summary of findings. 2000 Oregon Population Survey Task Force. http://egov.oregon.gov/DAS/OPB/docs/PopSurv/2000Summ.PDF. (January 26, 2009).

Washington Farm Bureau. 2008. Washington Farm Bureau mission statement. http://www.wsfb.com/about/history. (January 16, 2009).

Washington Secretary of State. 2004. 2004 federal general election results by county. http://www.vote.wa.gov/Elections/Results/ResultsByCounty.aspx?e=a3501711-c318-45f4-8a03-1d926ac839b7&j=a077943e-44ef-4b4e-b051-34b41c48179b&o=7b5d7925-77f3-4363-9c1c-0bc6d285a739. (April 9, 2009).

Washington Secretary of State. 2006a. Initiative measure 933. http://vote.wa.gov/Elections/VotersGuide/Measure.aspx?a=933&c=1. (January 28, 2009).

Washington Secretary of State. 2006b. General election results. http://www.vote.wa.gov/Elections/General/ResultsSummaryMeasures.aspx. (January 16, 2009).

Chapter 3: The Influence of Measure 37 Claims on Voting Shifts Between Measure 37 and Measure 49

Garrett Chrostek[2]

Introduction

The fundamental right to private property enjoyed by U.S. citizens and other legal entities is rooted in the 5th and 14th Amendments to the Constitution. Such a strong emphasis on the rights of the individual often creates conflict when policymakers pursue legislation in the greater public interest. As a result, there has been a perpetual cycle throughout our history concerning how society balances individual private property rights with perceptions of the public interest. As conditions in our social, political, and economic environments change, so has our assessment of which of these two competing values deserves greater priority. Changes in our values and priorities are manifested in who achieves political office, judicial rulings, and the laws and policies that are enacted. In Oregon, the strategic practice of using the ballot to determine the balance between these competing values has been a recurring theme. In the past 10 years, Oregon voters have faced three ballot initiatives concerning property rights. Oregonians passed Measure 7 in 2000 and Measure 37 in 2004. Both measures received strong support and passed with 53 percent and 61 percent of the vote, respectively. Yet after passage of Measure 37, Oregonians seemed to have had a change of heart and passed Measure 49 during a special election in November 2007, which substantially scaled back specific rights ordained by Measure 37. Measure 49 also received strong support and passed with 62 percent of the vote. Such a drastic shift might serve as an indication that Oregonians had revised their weighting in the balance between property rights and the public interest.

Although this balancing of values likely will continue to oscillate in the future, the apparent reversal of purpose in the minds of voters between Measures 37 and 49 provides an opportunity to examine what factors might shape public perceptions of that balance. Socioeconomic factors have long been identified and reported in the literature as having a measurable influence on voting on a variety of environmental issues. In this chapter, I examine the factors unique to Oregon that have changed between the passage of Measure 37 in 2004 and Measure 49 in 2007 and consider their potential influence in the realignment of voting by Oregonians.

The apparent reversal of purpose in the minds of voters between Measures 37 and 49 provides an opportunity to examine what factors might shape public perceptions of that balance.

---

[2] Garrett Chrostek is a J.D. candidate, 2012, Vermont Law School, 164 Chelsea Street, PO Box 96, South Royalton, VT 05068.

Measure 37 gave Oregon property owners (meeting certain qualifications) the right to file claims seeking compensation for economic losses resulting from land use regulations or receive a waiver of those regulations on their property. Measure 37 claims and their potential implications for exurban sprawl, agricultural land loss, and neighboring property owners became the center of intense public debate. To resolve differences in interpretations of Measure 37, Governor Kulongoski appointed the Big Look Task Force to elicit and consider public comments on Measure 37. Testimony presented to the Big Look Task Force revealed that many people did not understand what they were voting for when they voted "yes" on 37. For example, people testified that they did not understand that Measure 37 would facilitate residential and commercial development on agricultural and other lands that had previously been ineligible for development by the state's land use planning system. A similar message was portrayed in advertisement promoting Measure 49. Television spots, mailers, and opinion pieces frequently described widespread confusion over Measure 37 and expressed dissatisfaction with specific local Measure 37 claims. This raises the question: Did the concentration of Measure 37 claims in particular counties and cities influence the divergent outcomes between Measure 37 and Measure 49 in those places? Did this influence have a positive or negative effect on voting results? Can the magnitude of this influence be measured at the precinct and county levels? Or is this voting outcome simply a product of traditional partisan and regional politics? To investigate these questions, I recount the history of private property rights debates in Oregon, review research literature regarding attitudes toward land use, and examine Measure 37 and 49 voting patterns in counties and precincts. Results of the analysis help to explain differences in the voting outcomes of the two measures and provide insights for policymakers seeking to improve voter satisfaction with Oregon's land use planning system.

Land Use Policy in Oregon

During the 1960s and 1970s, the United States was in a period of strong emphasis on the "public interest." Demand for environmental protection inspired passage of the Nation's most significant environmental legislation, including the Clean Air Act (1963), the Endangered Species Act (1973), and the Clean Water Act (1977). This legislation significantly restricted the economic activities of private property owners in exchange for gains to the public good from a safer and healthier environment. The emphasis on the public interest also was evident in Oregon with passage of the Oregon Beach Bill (1967) and Senate Bill 100 (1973), which became the basis of Oregon's land use planning system—the first statewide comprehensive land use planning system in the United States. Oregon land use planning assigned zoning designations to individual properties dictating permissible land uses within zones. Through these regulations, the state aimed to serve the general welfare by protecting the state's agricultural economy and to promote the health of citizens by separating harmful industrial activities from residential areas. The legislation also aimed to curb urban sprawl and its associated environmental problems by concentrating development within urban-growth boundaries. However, to realize these benefits, private property owners had to accept significant limitations on the uses of their property.

Despite curtailing some individual private property rights, Senate Bill 100 was popular among the state's citizens and powerful agricultural interests. Oregon had experienced rapid suburban development during the 1960s, which posed a threat to the profitability of agriculture and citizens' enjoyment of open spaces. These concerns initially inspired public support for land use planning. Since implementation of planning, however, as Oregon's population continued to increase and its economy gradually became more service oriented, many private property owners became more resentful of the regulations imposed by planning. Private property interests began to mobilize, engaging in legal challenges to Senate Bill 100 based on the protections found in the 5th and 14th Amendments of the U.S. Constitution. Most challenges were dismissed as Senate Bill 100 was found to support a legitimate public purpose and meet other legal tests of takings law.

The Constitution and related federal court cases merely established a floor for minimum protections afforded to private property rights. States, by virtue of the 10th Amendment, were authorized to increase the level of private property rights protection, and, in a number of instances, they have. An initial effort to increase private property rights protection in Oregon occurred when Measure 7 passed in 2000. Measure 7 was a state constitutional amendment providing compensation to landowners when certain land use regulations reduced the fair market value of property. Following passage, Measure 7 was struck down by the Oregon Supreme Court in *League of Oregon Cities et al. v. State of Oregon et al.* (2002) because the measure addressed two separate state constitutional issues—adjusting the threshold for just compensation and regulating free speech by prohibiting compensation for regulations pertaining to pornography—which the Court found to be unconstitutional. Measure 7 was revived as a statutory initiative under Measure 37 to achieve the same goals but avoid similar constitutional challenge. Measure 37 passed in 2004 with 61 percent of the vote. Following passage, the constitutionality of the measure was challenged by pro-planning interests in Marion County, and the Circuit Court subsequently struck it down because it so severely infringed upon the state's police powers. An appeal was expedited to the State Supreme Court (*Macpherson et al. v. State of Oregon et al.* 2006) where the decision of the lower court was overturned.

Measure 37 accomplished two things for private property owners. First, it lowered the threshold for making claims for regulatory takings. Second, it developed a new avenue for administrative relief. However, Measure 37 did not apply to all landowners and could not provide relief from all regulations. In particular, Measure 37 only applied to landowners whose property has been owned within their family before the regulation causing the reduced property value was instituted. Compensation did not extend to federal regulations, regulations providing for the health and safety of the population, regulation associated with public nuisances identified in common law, and restrictions on businesses associated with adult entertainment. The avenue for administrative relief—commonly referred to as a "Measure 37 claim"—gave landowners 2 years to file. Claims were to be submitted to the government entity that had imposed the regulation resulting in reduction of fair market value. Claimants were also permitted to appeal decisions on their claim to the county circuit court. During the 2 years following passage of Measure 37, 7,717 claims were filed involving nearly 800,000 acres. Most claims involved subdivisions or partitions of high-value farm and forest lands. A majority were located in the Willamette Valley where most of the state's population resides (Portland State University 2007).

Immediately following passage of Measure 37, Democrats in the state legislature indicated that they would attempt to amend Measure 37. After failing to pass legislation amending the measure during the 2005 and 2007 sessions, the state legislature put a proposed amendment to the measure on the ballot, which became Measure 49. Measure 49 passed with 61 percent of the vote in a 2007 special election and significantly curtailed the size and scope of Measure 37 claims, and revised the available forms of compensation and the transferability of successful claims. Measure 49 disallows compensation for denied industrial or commercial development on high-value farm or forest lands and lands designated as critical ground-water areas. Compensation also is disallowed for subdivision requests of greater than 10 houses and for regulations that simply **restrict** rather than effectively **prohibit** development. Many of Oregon's land use regulations restrict industrial, commercial, or residential development by attaching certain conditions under which development is permissible. One example is the "farm income test" under which landowners who own less than 80 acres zoned for exclusive farm use are prevented from constructing new buildings unless they generate $80,000 or more in gross income from agricultural activities. However, although not a prohibition on development, many landowners are unable to meet the income test given agricultural market conditions, such that the end effect often is to prevent development. Still, because the income test does not explicitly prohibit building construction, landowners are unable to seek compensation for this regulation. Landowners also cannot seek compensation for regulations involving critical ground-water areas. Under Oregon law, landowners can withdraw up to 15,000 gallons a day for residential uses regardless of its availability. To protect critical ground-water areas from being overdrawn owing to increased residential expansion, Measure 49 prohibits landowners from seeking compensation for restrictions on development within these areas. Lastly, Measure 37 did not address the issue of transferability of successful claims. If a claim was successful, it was not clear under Measure 37 whether a landowner could transfer property with newly granted rights to a developer, another individual, or even a family member. Measure 49 allowed properties with successful claims to be transferred to any party provided the new party acts upon the claim within 10 years. In all, Measure 49 did not nullify Measure 37, but rather did significantly curtail it by limiting the amount of potential compensation possible and reducing the number of eligible claimants.

Literature Review

The underlying themes associated with Measures 37 and 49 involve public attitudes toward land use, growth, development, private property rights, and partisanship. Many of these attitudes are associated with socioeconomic characteristics that are commonly used to explain voting outcomes. One particular attitude—commonly referred to as NIMBYism—is central to investigating related research questions and requires particular attention.

NIMBY—"not in my backyard"—is an acronym used to describe an attitude of resistance to locating undesirable facilities in proximity to an individual's or group's residence, community, place of work, or any other area with which that person or group holds a favorable connection. It is a concept with deep roots in literature examining hostility toward development of polluting industries and other nuisance-producing facilities, such as nuclear powerplants, landfills, prisons, and mental health institutions (e.g., Furuseth and O'Callaghan 1991, Gameson and Modigliani 1989, Gordon and Gordon 1990, Nadel 1995). Although it is understandable that people do not want these sorts of developments near their place of residence, such attitudes have been documented to produce social costs when allowed to steer public policy. Regardless of personal preferences regarding the placement of such facilities, all citizens nonetheless require their services. Preventing undesirable

The underlying themes associated with Measures 37 and 49 involve public attitudes toward land use, growth, development, private property rights, and partisanship.

forms of development to locate in proximity to a community because of aesthetic or social preferences can increase the costs of delivering their associated services by increasing transportation costs or permitting demand to go unfulfilled. Unfulfilled demand forces community members to use inferior or less efficient substitutes for services, which can be associated with their own set of externalities. Although the NIMBY concept has been used to explain a variety of policy decisions and voting outcomes, it has previously not been applied to the preservation of natural amenities from residential development in a voting context.

Individuals or groups exhibit NIMBYistic characteristics when they perceive development of an undesirable facility as a threat to their security, economic position, or quality of life (Gameson and Modigliani 1989, Gordon and Gordon 1990). Similar themes are at the core of the Measure 37 debate, as exemplified by testimony to the Big Look Task Force. Measure 37 opponents, for example, described their unwillingness to allow farm and forest lands to be converted to residential developments whether it be on neighboring property or generally. Measure 37 opponents attributed the quality of life in Oregon to the state's land use planning system and viewed Measure 37 as a threat.

In contrast, critics of Oregon's land use planning system described land use policies as an elitist institution that unjustly restricts economic activity while contributing to housing problems by artificially inflating prices. Claims of elitism made by Measure 37 proponents are somewhat supported by research as income and education tend to be the dominant factors for predicting attitudes toward land use, growth, and development. For example, Green et al. (1996) found income and education to be the best predictors of support for land use regulations, both exhibiting positive correlation with regulation support. Similar results were found by Inman and McLeod (2002) whose survey of rural Wyoming residents found higher levels of education and seasonal residency were positively associated with higher levels of support for public management of private lands. Yet not all "elites" demonstrate similar patterns of support. Green et al. (1996) also found that high-income seasonal residents were more supportive of land use regulations because they are not connected to the economic benefits of growth and want to preserve their "special places." However, high-income permanent residents were less supportive because they were more connected to the economic benefits of growth.

Income and education also are highly associated with partisanship, which would help to explain partisan differences in attitudes toward land use regulations. Chapin and Connerly (2004) noted distinct differences in support for land use regulations in Florida between Republicans and Democrats. Republicans tend to be less accepting of government intervention in the economy and were found to be less supportive of Florida's growth management policies. In contrast, Democrats tend to place greater faith in government to solve social problems and are more supportive of policies to protect the environment (Van Liere and Dunlap 1980), which is one of the primary goals of Oregon's land use planning system.

Also important to the discussion of attitudes toward land use and analysis of voting patterns are the effects of rurality. Politics in Oregon frequently are premised on the "two states" theory, which hypothesizes political and cultural differences between the more urbanized Willamette Valley and the more rural remainder of the state as a source of conflict in state politics. Rural voters have long been associated with strong support for property rights and opposition to government intervention in the economy. Jackson-Smith et al. (2005) found that rural residents who held strong economic ties to their land demonstrated higher levels of resistance to land use regulation. However, recent increases in inmigration have begun to soften these traditional views on land use as rural areas become home to new residents from other (often urban) places. Smith and Krannich (2000) found long-term residents in high-amenity Rocky Mountain West locales to be more supportive of land use laws to protect the traditional economic base. Long-term residents were found to view tourism-related growth as only bringing seasonal employment and more expensive real estate. Short-term seasonal residents exhibited greater preference for growth to provide additional services and shopping opportunities. Yet when faced with declining prosperity in traditional economic activities, rural residents have been documented to revert to their traditional attitudes toward land use (Chapin and Connerly 2004).

Strong property rights sentiments also have been associated with areas dominated by public ownership of land (Musacchio et al. 2003). Fifty-seven percent of land in Oregon is under public ownership, with the highest concentrations in mountainous and high desert counties of Curry (69 percent) and Harney (75 percent). Counties with lower proportions of public land are located in the Willamette Valley, including Polk (12 percent), and in the grain-producing region of Gilliam (11 percent), Sherman (9 percent), and Morrow (22 percent). Lower levels of public land within counties reflect larger quantities of land suitable for agriculture. Musacchio et al. (2003) noted that people in areas comprising less public land may perceive greater scarcity of open space and other lands providing recreation opportunities and so tend to be more supportive of policies to protect lands that offer open space benefits. An association between open space scarcity and public demand or willingness to protect undeveloped lands also is found in studies of political support and voting on ballot measures that provide funds to farm, forest, and other open space lands (e.g., Kline 2006, Kline and Wichelns 1994).

Although these previous studies offer insight into individuals' attitudes toward land use regulations, research literature offers little insight regarding voting on land-use-related ballot initiatives and how and why it can change over time from one initiative to another. Voting on Measures 37 and 49 provide a unique opportunity to investigate factors in the shift in vote between two land use ballot initiatives.

Data, Hypotheses, and Methods

The foregoing analysis examines factors hypothesized to influence differences in voting outcomes of Measures 37 and 49 at both county and voting precinct levels. County observations include all 36 Oregon counties. Precinct-level observations include all voting precincts from three counties—Benton, Jackson, and Lane— representing different combinations of voting outcomes for Measure 37 and Measure 49: "yes-yes," "yes-no," and "no-yes," No county voted "no-no," Data availability weighed more heavily as a criterion for selecting these counties than did procuring a representative sample. Most counties in Oregon do not have precinct-level geographic information system (GIS) data describing Measure 37 claims, which was essential to the analysis. Precincts in Oregon also present other data limitations as the state's mail-in ballot system has rendered precincts effectively irrelevant. Although redistricting occurs for various elected offices, there is no longer any need to redraw precinct boundaries to keep them relatively proportional. As a result, census tracts do not follow precinct boundaries making it difficult to attribute socioeconomic data to individual precincts. To overcome this limitation, areal interpolation was used to fit socioeconomic data from census tracts to voting precincts. Precinct maps were combined with census tract boundaries to identify which tracts fall into which precincts. Socioeconomic data for each precinct then were computed using spatial averages. Similar methods have been used by the U.S. Census Bureau to fit demographic data to precincts in other states.

The analysis sought to examine factors that influenced why Oregonians voted in two different directions on two ballot measures concerning essentially the same underlying issue—balancing property rights versus public interest. Of interest is the shift in support for either a "public interest" perspective ("no" on 37 and "yes" on 49) or a pro-property rights perspective ("yes" on 37 and "no" on 49) within political boundaries. The dependent variable—shift in vote—was constructed as the difference between the percentage of "yes" votes for Measure 49 and "no" votes for Measure 37. For example, if a county voted 60 percent "yes" for Measure 49 and 30 percent "no" for Measure 37, then the county experienced a 30 percent shift in vote. An alternative specification based on the difference between "yes" votes on Measure 37 and "no" votes on Measure 49 would yield identical values.

> The analysis sought to examine factors that influenced why Oregonians voted in two different directions on two ballot measures concerning essentially the same underlying issue—balancing property rights versus public interest.

Two competing theories emerge for explaining the divergent outcomes of the Measure 37 and Measure 49 votes. The first theory—the NIMBY theory—suggests that Oregon voters voted consistent with reducing the threat they associated with Measure 37 claims in their communities. This theory assumes that Measure 37 claims are the primary predictor of shift in vote, with greater support for Measure 49 in places where claim activity was more prevalent. A second theory—the two-states theory—suggests that differences in support for statewide growth management policies are based on major political party affiliation and rural versus urban populations. This theory assumes that after Oregon voters became better educated about the implications of Measure 37, they voted in patterns more consistent with traditional regional and partisan factions more characteristic of the "two states" view of Oregon politics, with rural voters strongly leaning Republican and urban voters leaning Democrat. Both theories guided the selection of explanatory variables tested in the empirical models.

Several explanatory variables characterizing the extent of Measure 37 claims within political boundaries were included to examine potential NIMBY effects. Following the assumption that most Oregonians did not like Measure 37 claims, the more claims or greater extent of claims within a political boundary, the more likely citizens would be to use their vote to prevent or disrupt Measure 37 claims. More claims within a political boundary also could result in greater awareness of claims among voters and thus greater opportunity for voters to develop unfavorable opinions toward Measure 37. Moreover, testimony delivered to the Big Look Task Force and rhetoric from politicians supporting Measure 49 suggest that small claims, such as constructing a second home, were more consistent with the true intention behind Measure 37. Waivers for big subdivisions covering large parcels, on the other hand, were not consistent with voters' intentions, and these tended to receive media attention and were the focus of testimony at the Big Look hearings. Measure 37 claims variables included the number of claims within political boundaries, acreage under claim, acreage under claim as a proportion of the total area, and the number of large claims (>100 acres), all of which were expected to be positively associated with the "shift in vote." An additional variable—the ratio of eligible voters to the number of claims—was expected to be negatively associated with the "shift in vote." Data describing Measure 37 claims within counties were from Portland State University's Measure 37 Database, whereas precinct-level data were provided by county planning and GIS offices.

Other explanatory variables align more with the two-states theory. For example, partisanship weighed heavily in the debate over Measure 49 especially after Democrats in the state legislature acted to amend Measure 37. The variable %Democrat, which measured the level of Democratic voter registration within political boundaries based on data voter registration, were acquired from county election offices. Given that the dependent variable measures the "shift in vote," the effect of partisanship conceivably could have a low magnitude.

Also related to the two-states theory is the percentage of land area under public ownership within political boundaries as reported by the National Outdoor Recreation Supply Information System (Betz 1997), which was expected to have a negative correlation with "shift in vote." Public land ownership within political boundaries determines the amount of land available for private uses. As Measures 37 and 49 address permissible land uses on private property, areas with higher levels of public ownership are more significantly affected because the limited amount of private land available is further restricted by land use laws. Similarly, rurality was hypothesized to be a factor, with rural political units expected to be more strongly in favor of increased protection of property rights and thus more favorable to Measure 37 and less favorable to Measure 49 (and lower shift in vote). Urban political units, on the other hand, were expected to have a higher shift in vote. At the county level, urban and rural were differentiated using the USDA's Economic Research Service rural-urban continuum (Economic Research Service 2004). Rural precincts were identified as containing more than 16,000 acres. An additional dummy variable identifying counties located within the Willamette Valley (Multnomah, Clackamas, Washington, Yamhill, Polk, Marion, Linn, Benton, and Lane) was included to distinguish Oregon's more urban counties from the more rural counties.

Lastly, socioeconomic variables included per capita income ($1000s of 1999 dollars) and education, measured as the percentage of the population 25 and over with a college degree. (U.S. Bureau of the Census 2000). Precinct-level income and education data were developed using aerial interpolation of street nodes. This technique uses a GIS to locate census tracts within voting precinct boundaries. Similar to the case with the %Democrat, conceivably the effect of the income and education variables could be limited given that the dependent variable measures the shift in vote. However, positive directional relationships were expected based on the assumption that most Oregonians did not fully understand the implications of Measure 37 and that as they gained more knowledge about it they likely voted in patterns more consistent with the socioeconomic tendencies described in the literature.

The explanatory variables and their expected direction of correlation with the shift in vote are presented in table 3.1. Bivariate correlations indicated potential relationships between variables associated with the first nine hypotheses and "shift in vote." Regression analysis using ordinary least squares was used to further understand the relationship among the variables. Akaike's Information Criterion (AIC) was employed to determine best fitting models. For the precinct-level analysis, separate models were estimated for each of the three counties of interest, including a best fit model and models encompassing the same variables to make comparisons across counties. Finally, an additional set of models were estimated that pooled observations from all three counties.

Results

County-Level Models

Descriptive statistics for the county observations are summarized in table 3-2. Bivariate analysis indicated that most of the directional relationships among the variables tested and shift in vote were consistent with hypothesized expectations (table 3-3). With the exception of the number of acres under claim, the number of large claims, and the ratio of eligible voters to claims, all correlations held some level of statistical significance (p < 0.05). The rural-urban continuum variable produced the largest absolute value for Pearson's r and the smallest p-value.

Regression analysis included four alternative model specifications. The M37 model included only those variables characterizing Measure 37 claim activity in

Table 3-1—Hypothesized direction of relationships, level of analysis, and supporting theory in predicting shift in vote

Variable	Predicted directional relationship	Level of analysis	Theory[a]
Acres under claim	+	Both	NIMBY
Number of claims	+	Both	NIMBY
Percentage of boundary under claims	+	Both	NIMBY
Large claims	+	Both	NIMBY
Ratio of eligible voters to claims	-	Both	NIMBY
Percentage of Democrats	+	Both	Two-states
Public land	-	County	Two-states
Rural-urban continuum	-	County	Two-states
Willamette Valley	+	County	Two-states
Rural	-	Precinct	Two-states
Education	+	Both	Two-states
Income	+	Both	Two-states

[a] NIMBY = not in my backyard.

Table 3-2—County descriptive statistics

Variable	No.	Minimum	Maximum	Mean	Standard deviation
Shift in vote (percent)	36	2.35	30.05	18.06	7.63
Acres under claim	36	0.00	64,466	22,012	18,960
Number of claims	36	1.00	1,076	212.89	246.29
Percentage of county under claims	36	0.00	13.93	2.29	2.73
Large claims	36	0.0	72.00	18.89	19.97
Ratio of eligible voters to claims	36	0.03	2.30	0.56	0.48
Percentage of Democrats	36	25.62	50.87	34.50	5.69
Public land (percent)	36	9.19	78.42	46.02	21.11
Rural-urban continuum	36	1.00	9.00	4.92	2.57
Education (percentage with bachelors degree)	36	11.00	47.40	19.18	19.97
Income	36	13.90	25.97	18.27	2.58

Table 3-3—County correlations with shift in vote

Variable	Pearson's r	P-value
Acres under claim	0.118	0.492
Number of claims	0.350	0.036*
Percentage of county under claims	0.415	0.012*
Large claims	0.157	0.359
Ratio of eligible voters to claims	0.114	0.509
Percentage of Democrats	0.520	0.001**
Public land	-0.445	0.007**
Rural-urban continuum	-0.563	0.000**
Education	0.330	0.049*
Income	0.437	0.008**

Note: The * and ** indicate that the correlation coefficient is statistically significant at 95 percent and 99 percent confidence level, respectively.

counties (table 3-4). Most of the estimated coefficients for these variables exhibited hypothesized directional relationships, with the exception of the number of claims and the number of large claims, although none of the estimated coefficients were found to be statistically significant ($p < 0.05$). The CONTROL model comprised the remaining variables not associated with Measure 37 claims activity. This model produced a significant F-value and yielded a larger adjusted R^2 than the M37 model, suggesting that Measure 37 claim activity variables are not the primary predictors of shift in vote. All explanatory variables held directional relationships consistent with hypotheses with the exception of education and income.

In the BEST FIT model, the Willamette Valley variable and the percentage of registered Democrats were the only statistically significant variables. These results suggest that shift in vote is best explained at the county level by the two-states

These results suggest that shift in vote is best explained at the county level by the two-states theory and associated effects of political party affiliation.

Table 3-4—Estimated regression coefficients for county-level voting models predicting shift in vote

Variable	M37	Control	Model 1	Best fit
Constant	16.184**	15.494	5.912	7.090
	(7.58)	(1.09)	(0.80)	(1.00)
Acres under claim	-0.000			
	(-1.31)			
Number of claims	0.009		-0.001	
	(1.13)		(-0.21)	
Percentage of county under claims	1.292		0.354	
	(1.97)		(0.70)	
Large claims	-0.021			
	(-0.21)			
Ratio of eligible voters to claims	0.632			2.571
	(0.23)			(1.27)
Percentage of Democrats		0.399	0.394*	0.445*
		(0.180)	(2.05)	(2.25)
Public land		-0.089	-0.078	-0.094
		(-1.78)	(-1.46)	(-1.90)
Rural-urban continuum		-0.675		
		(-1.08)		
Willamette Valley		6.300	6.346	8.676**
		(1.75)	(1.96)	(2.70)
Education		-0.178		-0.192
		(-0.79)		(-1.08)
Income		-0.000		
		(-0.014)		
No.	36	36	36	36
R-squared (R^2)	0.251	0.527	0.496	0.532
Adjusted R^2	0.126	0.430	0.412	0.454
Degrees of Freedom	29	29	30	30
F-statistic	2.01	5.39**	5.90**	6.81**
Akaike's Information Criterion			132.60	129.95

Note: The t-statistics are in parentheses. The * and ** indicate that the correlation coefficient is statistically significant at 95 percent and 99 percent confidence level, respectively.

theory and associated effects of political party affiliation. It is plausible that voters did not fully understand what the implications of Measure 37 would be and took cues from their party or their elected officials—disproportionately Democratic in the Willamette Valley and Republican in the rest of the state—when voting on Measure 49. Education had a negative directional relationship but was statistically insignificant. The ratio of eligible voters to claims was the only Measure 37 variable included in this model, but also was statistically insignificant. As the BEST FIT model offered little insight into the effects of measures of Measure 37 claim activity, MODEL I also was included in Table 3-4 as it represents the next-best-fitting model that included more than one Measure 37 variable. The percentage of the county under claim was the strongest predictor of shift in vote among the

Measure 37 variables in this model although it was not statistically significant. The percentage of Democrats was the only significant variable in this model, and it displayed the expected positive directional relationship.

Precinct-Level Models

Although the three sample counties from which precinct-level data were drawn are not necessarily representative of a majority of counties in the state, county averages for key variables were roughly comparable to statewide averages across counties, including shift in vote, the percentage of the precinct under claim, the percentage of registered Democrats, and per capita income (table 3-5). Education levels for the sample counties were greater than the state average across all counties. Bivariate correlations produced different results compared to correlations using county-level data. All of the measures of Measure 37 claim activity had directional relationships conflicting with the hypotheses (table 3-6) with the exception of the ratio of eligible voters to claims, which does not support the NIMBY theory. The percentage of registered Democrats, education, and per capita income held positive relationships as predicted. The differences in directional relationships between the county- and precinct-level models suggest that those voters closest to Measure 37 claims were less influenced by claims and had a lower shift in vote.

Several precinct-level models were tested, with table 3-7 containing the best fitting model for each county. These models suggest differences across the three sample counties in the factors that may have influenced the shift in vote. Rurality and income were the best predictors of shift in vote in Benton County, as both held statistically significant negative relationships. The ratio of eligible voters to claims was the only Measure 37-related variable retained, but its estimated coefficient was not statistically significant ($p > 0.05$). Jackson County data did not produce a better

Table 3-5—Sample county voting precinct descriptive statistics

Variable	No.	Minimum	Maximum	Mean	Standard deviation
Shift in vote (percent)	154	-5.92	46.30	16.75	11.77
Acres under claim	154	0.00	13,986	535	1,382
Number of claims	154	0.00	81.00	7.06	13.00
Percentage of precinct under claims	154	0.00	16.45	1.45	2.93
Large claims	154	0.00	27.00	1.42	3.15
Ratio of eligible voters to claims	154	0.00	5.95	0.47	0.87
Percentage of Democrats	154	23.63	61.78	38.83	8.49
Education (percentage with bachelors degree)	154	5.20	80.59	27.91	15.46
Income	154	7.65	33.94	20.25	43.91

Table 3-6—Precinct correlations with shift-in-vote

Variable	Pearson's r	P-value
Acres under claim	-1.125	0.122
Number of claims	-0.294	0.000**
Percentage of county under claims	-0.133	0.099
Large claims	-0.137	0.089
Ratio of eligible voters to claims	-0.305	0.000**
Percentage of Democrat	0.605	0.000**
Education	0.369	0.000**
Income	0.008	0.917

Note: The * and ** indicate that the correlation coefficient is statistically significant at 95 percent and 99 percent confidence level, respectively.

Table 3-7—Estimated regression coefficients for best-fit voting precinct models for shift in vote in three counties

Variable	Benton	Jackson	Lane
Constant	46.935**	-14.891**	34.307**
	(5.23)	(-3.79)	(16.85)
Acres under claim			
Number of claims			
Percentage of precinct under claims			.398*
			(2.27)
Large claims			
Ratio of eligible voters to claims	-2.475		-1.954
	(-1.60)		(-1.28)
Percentage of Democrats		.537**	
		(4.64)	
Rural	-6.336*		-3.830**
	(-2.25)		(-2.75)
Education			.065
			(1.71)
Income	-.891*		-.549**
	(-2.25)		(-4.84)
No.	20	51	83
R-squared (R^2)	.571	.305	.429
Adjusted R^2	.490	.291	.392
Degrees of Freedom	16	49	77
F-statistic	7.04**	21.49**	11.58**
Akaike's Information Criterion	70.27	196.27	232.90

Note: The t-statistics are in parentheses. The * and ** indicate that the correlation coefficient is statistically significant at 95 percent and 99 percent confidence level, respectively.

fitting model and only consisted of two parameters. The percentage of registered Democrats yielded a positive relationship as hypothesized. For Lane County, income and rurality were important explanatory variables similar to Benton County. The percentage of the precinct under claim had a statistically significant positive relationship and was one of two instances in the entire study in which a

Measure 37 claim variable yielded this hypothesized result. Income and rurality had statistically significant negative relationships in the Lane County model.

Observations from all three of the sample counties were combined in a final set of models, which were specified to parallel the earlier county-level models (table 3-8). One precinct in Jackson County did not have GIS data available and was therefore excluded from this analysis. Similar to results from the county-level models, the CONTROL model produced a greater adjusted R^2 than the M37 model suggesting that greater variation in the shift in vote is explained by the control variables rather than the measures of Measure 37 claim activity. In the M37 model, the number of claims yielded statistically significant negative relationships, contrary to the expected directional relationships, whereas the ratio of eligible voters to claims held a statistically significant negative relationship as expected. This would again

Table 3-8—Estimated regression coefficients for voting models for predicting shift in vote for all precincts

Variable	M37	Control	Model 1	Best fit
Constant	19.188**	-9.956	19.569**	17.027**
	(18.07)	(-1.65)	(4.81)	(4.85)
Acres under claim	0.000			
	(.18)			
Number of claims	-0.468**			
	(3.17)			
Percentage of precinct under claims	-0.103		0.172	
	(-0.31)		(1.08)	
Large claims	1.513			
	(1.76)			
Ratio of eligible voters to claims	-2.845*		0.157	
	(-2.01)		(0.21)	
Jackson			-18.556**	-18.417**
			(-15.61)	(-16.25)
Percentage of Democrats		0.784**	0.253**	0.304**
		(6.53)	(3.18)	(4.64)
Rural		-0.185	-3.083*	-2.974**
		(-0.11)	(-2.31)	(-2.95)
Education		0.061	0.062	
		(0.76)	(1.26)	
Income		-0.265	-0.368**	-0.243*
		(-1.18)	(-2.64)	(-2.30)
No.	154	154	154	154
R-squared (R^2)	0.158	0.372	0.777	0.773
Adjusted R^2	0.13	0.355	0.766	0.767
Degrees of Freedom	148	149	146	149
F-statistic	5.57**	22.09**	72.45**	126.66**
Akaike's Information Criterion			543.684	540.239

Note: The t-statistics are in parentheses. The * and ** indicate that the correlation coefficient is statistically significant at 95 percent and 99 percent confidence level, respectively.

suggest that those voters closest to the claims were less influenced by Measure 37 claims and therefore were less likely to experience a shift in vote. In the CONTROL model only the percentage of registered Democrats was statistically significant, but the rurality and education did exhibit directional relationships consistent with the county-level model.

To correct problems of autocorrelation, a dummy variable for Jackson County was included in the MODEL I and BEST FIT models. The percentage of registered Democrats and rurality were two of the four statistically significant predictors of shift in vote in MODEL I, similar to results from the county-level analysis. The other statistically significant variables were the Jackson County dummy variable and per capita income, both of which held statistically significant negative relationships. A negative relationship with Jackson County is consistent with the county's descriptive statistics where the mean shift in vote is substantially lower than Benton and Lane Counties. None of the measures of Measure 37 activity were statistically significant, but all exhibited positive directional relationships. The BEST FIT model provides further evidence for the two states theory, as this model only consisted of the percentage of Democrats, rural, income, and the Jackson County variables, all of which were statistically significant. There were no changes in the directional relationships of the variables between the MODEL I and BEST FIT models. The BEST FIT model had more degrees of freedom compared to MODEL I, which increased the t-statistics on all of the parameters with the exception of income. The F-statistic was also substantially greater in the BEST FIT model in comparison to MODEL I.

Conclusions and Policy Implications

This study sought to identify factors that influenced the divergent voting outcomes of Measures 37 and 49. Although much of the media attention during both campaigns focused on specific Measure 37 claims, empirical evidence supporting the NIMBY theory as an explanation of voting shifts is not strongly supported by this analysis as measures of claim activity were not significant predictors of the shift in vote between Measures 37 and 49 at either county or precinct levels (table 3-9). Results provide greater support for the two states theory as the Measure 37 controversy helped to accentuate differences in land use regulation and property rights perspectives between urban and rural populations and between Democrats and Republicans. In particular, rurality and Democratic voter registration were significant predictors of shift in vote at both county and precinct levels of analysis and were the most consistent variables in terms of directional relationships (table 3-9).

Table 3-9—Summary of predicted directional relationships and results for shift in vote model parameters

Variable	Predicted directional relationship	Level of analysis	Theory[a]	Supported by results
Acres under claim	+	Both	NIMBY	No
Number of claims	+	Both	NIMBY	No
Percentage of boundary under claims	+	Both	NIMBY	No
Large claims	+	Both	NIMBY	No
Ratio of eligible voters to claims	-	Both	NIMBY	Yes
Percentage of Democrats	+	Both	Two states	Yes
Public land	-	County	Two states	No
Rural-urban continuum	-	County	Two states	Yes
Willamette Valley	+	County	Two states	Yes
Rural	-	Precinct	Two states	Yes
Education	+	Both	Two states	No
Income	+	Both	Two states	No

[a] NIMBY = not in my backyard.

These results do not rule out the possibility that Measure 37 claims influenced individual voters. Rather, they suggest that the concentration of claims within particular political units cannot be linked to voting patterns based on the variables used and the counties examined in this study. Further inquiry could draw on additional GIS data, should it become available, to examine a more representative sample of counties. Analysis of the income and education variable also could be extended by using U.S. census blocks or block groups for areal interpolation. Further research also could evaluate the association of Measure 37 claim activity and levels of voter turnout, as well as the potential influence of various media. Inquires into the influence of campaign spending might shed additional light on the conflicting outcomes of the Measure 37 and Measure 49 votes. Finally, future analysis might incorporate a variable for the number of Measure 37 claims that moved forward with development in a political boundary.

Findings from this study offer insights for policymakers seeking to increase voter satisfaction with Oregon's land use planning system. Rural areas with fewer registered Democrats demonstrate less opposition to Measure 37 claims, and a number of such precincts (primarily in Jackson County) experienced a negative shift in vote. Such results suggest that these areas tend to favor maintenance of property rights over protection of public interest. To appease this population, the state could consider moving away from statewide land use goals to pursue development strategies tailored for particular regions. Although rural areas with low Democratic voter registration seek deregulation, the largely privately owned Willamette Valley appears more favorable to public regulation of private lands. Maintenance of development restrictions in support of the public good seems to align with voter satisfaction in this region.

There are also important implications for interest groups on different sides of the Oregon land use planning debate. Supporters of Measure 37 initiated their campaign to seek relief from what they believed to be overly burdensome land use regulation. Although Measure 49 offers a reprieve from certain regulations to select landowners, it will not fully satisfy people frustrated with the entire land use planning system. As population increases and rural areas look to move away from development strategies based on agriculture, the debate will likely resurface. Ideally, both supporters and detractors of Oregon's land use planning system would work together to forge a compromise vision to head off future iterations of the Measure 37 debate. Measure 37 and 49 outcomes also show the important role that information plays in shaping political support for ballot initiatives. The passage of Measure 49 on the heels of Measure 37 suggests that voters may not have fully understood the ramifications of Measure 37 based on the information they had at the time of voting.

Beyond identifying what happened between the Measure 37 and Measure 49 votes, it is important to understand what this vote means in the greater debate over the balance between private property rights and the public interest in Oregon. Measure 49 is the first substantial indication of a directional shift in this balance since society began to favor private property rights in the 1980s. However, it is yet to be determined whether Measure 49 demarks an actual realignment of perspective or merely a temporary oscillation. A better understanding will be available after the next major property-rights-related legislation or court outcome. Yet with Democrats gaining control of both chambers of the state legislature and more engaged Democratic voters, the signs point toward a period of greater emphasis on the public interest.

Ideally, both supporters and detractors of Oregon's land use planning system would work together to forge a compromise vision to head off future iterations of the Measure 37 debate.

Acknowledgments

This research was conducted by the author in partial fulfillment of a Masters of Public Policy, Department of Political Science, Oregon State University. Partial funding was provided by the Department of Political Science. The author thanks Drs. Roger Hammer, Brent Steel, and Robert Sahr for guidance and helpful comments.

References

Betz, C.J. 1997. NORSIS 1997: Codebook and documentation. Athens, GA: U.S. Department of Agriculture, Forest Service, Southern Research Station. http://www.srs.fs.usda.gov/trends/norsiscode.pdf. (March 11, 2010).

Chapin, T.S.; Connerly, C.E. 2004. Attitudes toward growth management in Florida. Journal of the American Planning Association. 70(4): 443–452.

Economic Research Service. 2004. Measuring rurality: rural-urban continuum codes. Washington, DC: U.S. Department of Agriculture. http://www.ers.usda.gov/Briefing/Rurality/RuralUrbCon/. (March 10, 2010).

Furuseth, O.J.; O'Callaghan, J. 1991. Community response to a municipal waste incinerator: NIMBY or neighbor? Landscape and Urban Planning. 21(3): 163–171.

Gameson, W.A.; Modigliani, A. 1989. Media discourse and public opinion on nuclear power: a constructionist approach. American Journal of Sociology. 95(1): 1–37.

Gordon, R.J.; Gordon, L. 1990. Neighborhood responses to stigmatized urban facilities: a private mental hospital and other facilities in Phoenix, Arizona. Journal of Urban Affairs. 12: 437–447.

Green, G.P.; Marcouiller, D.; Deller, S.; Erkkila, D.; Sumathi, N.R. 1996. Local dependency, land use attitudes, and economic development: comparisons between seasonal and permanent residents. Rural Sociology. 61(3): 427–443.

Inman, K.; McLeod, D.M. 2002. Property rights and public interests: a Wyoming agricultural lands study. Growth and Change. 33(1): 91–114.

Jackson-Smith, D.; Kreuter, U.; Krannich, R. 2005. Understanding the multidimensionality of property rights orientations: evidence from Utah and Texas ranchers. Society and Natural Resources. 18: 587–610.

Kline, J.D. 2006. Public demand for preserving local open space. Society and Natural Resources. 19(7): 645–659.

Kline, J.D.; Wichelns, D. 1994. Using public referendum data to characterize support for purchasing development rights to farmland. Land Economics. 70(2): 223–233.

League of Oregon Cities et al. v. State of Oregon et al. 2002. 334 Ore. 645; 56 P.3d 892.

Macpherson et al. v. State of Oregon et al. 2006. 340 Ore. 117; 130 P.3d 308.

Musacchio, L.; Crewe, K.; Steiner, F.; Schmidt, J. 2003. The future of agricultural landscape preservation in the Phoenix metropolitan region. Landscape Journal. 22(2): 140–154.

Nadel, B.A. 1995. Prison sightings: a rundown of the factors that go into site selection and development of correctional facilities. Planning. 61(6): 2–3.

Portland State University. 2007. Measure 37 database. Portland, OR. http://www.pdx.edu/ims/measure-37-database. (July 1, 2009).

U.S. Bureau of the Census. 2000. United States census 2000. Washington, DC: U.S. Department of Commerce. http://www.census.gov/main/www/cen2000.html (March 10, 2010).

Smith, M.D.; Krannich, R.S. 2000. Culture clash revisited: newcomer and longer-term residents' attitudes toward land use, development, and environmental issues in rural communities in the Rocky Mountain West. Rural Sociology. 65(3): 396–421.

Van Liere, K.D.; Dunlap, R.E. 1980. The social basis of environmental concern: a review of hypotheses, explanations, and empirical evidence. Public Opinion Quarterly. 44(2): 181–197.